OTHER SIDE OF THE MEDAL

EDWARD JOHN THOMPSON

GYAN

Published by

Gyan Publishing House
5, Ansari Road
Daryaganj, New Delhi-110002
Phone: 011-47034999, 9811692060
E-mail: books@gyanbooks.com

Distribution Network
gyanbooks.com
India, USA, Canada, UK, Australia

ISBN: 978-93-7225-118-0 (PB)

First Published, 1902

2nd Impression 2025

Printed at: Gyan Press, Delhi.

OTHER SIDE OF THE MEDAL
Arthur: EDWARD JOHN THOMPSON

OTHER SIDE OF THE MEDAL

Owing to the antiquity and rarity of this book, certain pages are regrettably absent, and readability is compromised due to the blurring of the original text. If you possess any insights regarding the availability of these missing sections, kindly inform us. Your assistance is crucial in ensuring the completion of this significant work for the benefit of future generations.

THE OTHER SIDE OF THE MEDAL

THE OTHER SIDE OF THE MEDAL

BY

EDWARD THOMPSON

THIRD EDITION

Published by
Leonard & Virginia Woolf at The Hogarth Press
52 Tavistock Square, London, W.C. 1

1930

PREFACE

This book has been long suppressed. To friends who urged that its publication would stir up bitter feelings, I point out that the deeds of which it speaks were done, and men's minds securely hold the smouldering memory. Other friends, among them some of the names most honoured in contemporary literature, have urged that the risk be taken. "Truth has an eternal title to our confession, though we are sure to be the sufferers by it." The book sets out matters that no Indian could, or perhaps should, set out, and I believe that it will change the attitude of every Englishman who reads it to the end. If that belief is justified, then I have no choice but to trust to the magnanimity of my own people, and to the magnanimity of that other people, in friendship with whom I have found so much happiness.

PREFACE TO SECOND EDITION

My countrymen in India have been generous to this book; and when journals of the strongly British traditions of the Lahore *Civil and Military*

Gazette and the Allahabad *Pioneer* welcome a statement as long overdue, the nervousness of Christian leaders in England who wrote privately expressing their deep sympathy, but doubting if the time was ripe and if the book would not " do harm " in India, is seen to have been unnecessary. I think that missionary leaders overvalue " Christian statesmanship "; truth and fairness are more essential parts of religion than even a wise expediency. There is a pharisaism in the attitude that is always seeking to " do good to others," and forgets duties that are closer to our own needs.

A fortnight before my book was published, the Lawrence statue at Lahore was again mutilated. The statue was then covered over, and reappeared six months later with a new inscription, " I have served you both with pen and sword." An old controversy is thereby laid to rest, and my note on the statue now has a historical interest only.

I have changed four misprints, and in one sentence have displaced the dangerous word " every." No other changes seem called for.

CONTENTS

CHAP.

I. Indian Irreconcilability 9

II. The Mutiny 26

III. Shadows of the Mutiny 84

IV. Conclusion 128

Appendix—

Note on Mutiny Literature 134

Personal Notes 136

THE OTHER SIDE OF THE MEDAL

CHAPTER I

INDIAN IRRECONCILABILITY

I

THEY say in Oxford to-day that the mention of the word *India* is guaranteed "to empty the smallest hall" in the city. Oxford is over-lectured, and its inhabitants are glutted with enlightenment. Yet, if we strip the epigram of exaggeration, a statement worth consideration remains. Oxford has known a line of Indian, and especially Sanskrit, scholars, who have been a noble part of its manifold greatness. But Indian studies are dying in England to-day, and interest in India seems almost dead. There is an impression that we have finished with India, and that, anyway, Indian pretensions of achievement in thought or poetry have been found out. The people of

India, we understand, are tired of our rule; they are ungrateful for what we have done for them. Very well, we will go. We can hold India still if we are prepared to shed sufficient blood; but the outcry over Amritsar has shown that we are not. More merciful than our fathers, we are not willing to wade through another Mutiny into a renewal of our lease, and we are disillusioned and weary from the war that has finished. So we are going —going bitterly and contemptuously. Our young men hang back from the Indian services. The famous Civil Service, which used to offer a career within the gift of no other country, no longer (we are told) attracts the pick of our universities, but with difficulty draws an intellectually poorer type of man, and that in extremely exiguous numbers. Indian thought, which a famous professor once upon a time almost induced our people to think a sun, is now seen to be a moon, pallid and shut in with watery mysticism. Indian literature is a gently pleasing patter about cows and lotuses.

And yet there are signs that, for all our unwillingness, India is going to compel our attention. Ireland has won the control of her destinies, the problems of Palestine and Irak are not yet ripe, that of Egypt has been shelved. India remains, unsatisfied, embittered, troublesome. The beginnings of constitutional government already accorded by us, and enlarged so generously (as we thought—not without reason), have been scornfully rejected, and the deliberative and legislative assemblies are a farce. Viceroys and Governors have to "certify" budgets thrown out by the people's elected representatives. Remembering what older troubles began with finance—the American Revolution, our own Civil War of King and Commonwealth, the rejected Budget which led to the House of Lords losing its power—and remembering, too, how public conviction, no less than the whole course of our history, justifies the taxpayer's claim to control expenditure, we cannot help but realise that the struggle is but at its commencement. However unwilling St George may be to be vexed with this Indian dragon, he is not going to escape it, for it is already moving, and there can be no doubt that its path and his are going to coincide, and soon.

II

British lack of interest in India is no new thing. It has been notorious, and a theme of savage comment by Indians, that the Indian Debate in the House of Commons has been regarded with indifference by the few who attended, with contempt by the many who stayed away. Sir Henry Fowler's noble appeal, that every member should consider himself a member for India, since India was disfranchised in the assembly that controlled her destinies, won a spectacular triumph when made, but has been forgotten since. Two years ago, a Member of Parliament of twenty years' standing asked a friend of mine, "What's happened to that fellow Gander—Gandy—or some such name, who used to give so much trouble? You never hear of him now"—thereby showing that it was possible to be a Privy Councillor and yet be ignorant that his greatest contemporary had gone to jail,[1] after a trial that to Indians had been something representative of themselves as no legislative assembly has yet been representative, a trial in which India (so they felt) had been judged and sentenced by an alien court. With what graceful light-heartedness doctrines that have turned the Indian world upside down are dismissed by our subtlest brains a recent trial has shown :

Mr Justice M'Cardie.—What is soul-force? (*Laughter.*)

Sir Walter Schwabe.—The view of Gandhi is that by peace and quiet methods and constant prayer, and by centring the soul on your object, you will attain that object.

Mr Justice M'Cardie (reading from the defendant's book, *Gandhi and Anarchy*).—I see that, according to the defendant's book, the first principle of Gandhi's belief is that all lawyers and all Courts should be dispensed with. (*Laughter.*)

---

[1] He was still in jail when the question was asked.

Sir Walter Schwabe.—That suggestion has many advantages.

Mr Justice M'Cardie.—You do not approve of his soul-force movement? (*Laughter.*)[1]

"There be three things which are too wonderful for me, yea, four which I know not: the way of an eagle in the air; the way of a serpent upon a rock; the way of a ship in the heart of the sea; and the way of a man with a maid."[2] And there are three kinds of humour which are too wonderful for the average man, but meet with immediate and vociferous recognition: the humour of a master in his class; the humour of a judge in his Court; and the humour of a general in his mess. How well such a passage as the one I have quoted recalls the happy days of the war! "I say, Major, have you heard the General's latest? He says the new orders from G.H.Q. remind him of the curate's egg—they are good in parts!" (*Laughter.*) "No? Did you really, sir? How absolutely topping! Perfectly priceless!" (*Laughter.*)

Our indifference, which it is so difficult to make Indians understand, has roots going very far back, and to us is explicable enough. India has never been quite "our job." It began for us as the concern of a private company of traders, and its

[1] Reported in the *Times*, 3rd May 1924.
[2] Proverbs, xxx. 18, 19.

administration passed from their hands into those of relatively a few families, who carried on the tradition from father to son, as civil servants or army officers. What had India to do with the great middle classes of Britain, except that they sent a few missionaries and an increasing number of business men, the latter for the most part haunting a few large towns—Calcutta, Bombay, Madras?

But to-day indifference is hardening into anger and dislike. We are "fed up" with India and Indians. A famous university professor remarked to me, "From all I can make out, we have done the greatest work in India that has ever been done by one country for another, and it has been received with nothing of gratitude." So, to sum up, Indians do not know when they are well off; they are seditious and envious and unthankful. Very well, we will go, being too proud and too decent to govern by massacre. But we know what we think of them, and we know very well what will happen to them as soon as we go—what an avalanche of plunder and rape will pour in, from the Gurkhas and the Moslem hordes of the north-west, to augment the internal yeast of commotion set in being by their own martial races, by Rajputs, Mahrattas, and Sikhs. Then the sleek Bengali lawyer will find out, too late, what we did for him, and the intriguing, proud Brahmin will wish he had not sowed this sword-crop! That will "larn them to be toads!" As an eloquent lady asked in the Calcutta *Statesman*, urging all right-minded people to contribute to the "Dyer Fund," "Have Indians forgotten how they were plundered and persecuted by self-seeking robbers and tyrants, in the evil days before the British bulldog pinned them to the dust? Those were dire days indeed!" Yes, Indians have been very foolish.

III

And, from time to time, expositions of the Indian attitude appear, each to be hailed as at last giving us the real truth about that perplexing person, the Hindu. It is surprising how much of each successive exposition is the most threadbare second-hand—surprising how much of it derives from Mr Kipling's brilliant and by no means wholly misleading caricatures of Indians. We are told about the "babu," and about the creature's parrot-like assimilation of words whose meaning he does not understand, and his absurd and laughable use of English. We are invited to be amused by the "Failed B.A." It is explained how foolish it was to give these people "education"—though the writers never explain how the vast, necessary army of underlings aware of English (and aware of it to some purpose, since their rulers rarely know any Indian language with any efficiency), without whom our Government could not carry on for a day, is to be obtained without "education." Then there is a great deal about "Pagett, M.P.," and his evil influence during those scandalous cold-weather trips of his; and a great deal about the wicked "Radicals" and the "sentimentalists" and "humanitarians," who hamper the good work of ruling India. The latest and (at the moment of writing this) most lauded of our enlighteners draws attention (at great length) "to the lonely and august figure of the mugwump,"[1] and gives us the "notes" by which we can identify the man who is in this unapostolic succession. "Racialism, patriotism, respect for national honour are anathema to him. The methods by which a healthy community will vindicate its rights, punish dissidents, suppress the foreign foe, are therefore in his view sinful."[1] The mugwump, this authority assures us, is so lost to all elementary decency that "the national ideals, the national religion"—even that, mark you! *tantum mugwumpietas potuit suadere malorum* —"the national morality, are all suspect to him."[1] It is a heavy charge.

We are often told, too, the kind of Englishman that the Indian loves and will follow to the fires of Tophet—the strong, silent "God's Englishman," taciturn, deep—unfathomably deep, and skilled in all the ways of the snaky Oriental. His words are few but pregnant; let his foes beware

[1] Al. Carthill, *The Lost Dominion*, pp. 72, 73.

of them, for they are but the prelude to his swift and terror-striking acts—the brief, warning snort of the rhinoceros before he charges through the jungle at his photographer. He is like Bunyan's Moses: "It was but a word and a blow, and he knocked me down." Lastly, it is explained that the Indian root of the trouble is the Brahmin. We are told of his pride, of his agelong ascendancy, and how, by adapting himself to each successive change of rule, he still kept the real power in his hands, until he was foiled by the efficiency and even justice of the unbribable Englishman. Now he is discontented, and he stokes the fires of "sedition." "This class may be figured under the imaginary character of Panditji."[1] The martial races—good, easy-going fellows, such as the Sikhs and jolly little Gurkhas—would be all right left to themselves. They are always "true to their salt"; they have no thought but for their regimental *izzat* and to serve the sahib they adore. From their ranks have come the "trusty servants" of countless thrilling boys' stories. When all their compatriots have turned into "swarthy devils," these splendid fellows have stopped bullets and knife-thrusts meant for their masters, and have died murmuring, "It all right, sahib. I happy—dying for master." And the

[1] For a detailed and brilliant exposure of Panditji's activities and a remorseless discovery of his inner mind, see *The Lost Dominion*, pp. 51 *seq.*

sahibs, pausing ere they pass on to renewed slaughter of the treacherous villains in front of them, wipe away a manly tear and say, "Poor Gopal! He was a good fellow, though he did worship false gods."

But the Brahmin—"God shield us! for there is not a more fearful wild-fowl than your Brahmin living; and we ought to look to't!" He flits about India, a vexed and vexing phantom; and he stirs up the simple folk about him, hoping that from those troubled waters he may be able to fish up again his lost dominion. Well, he will discover his error, as we have seen. Once upon a time, Indian legend tells us, the Gods and Demons churned the Ocean to recover the lost nectar of immortality. They recovered it, but from that churning emerged poison also, which threatened the lives of all creatures. So will it prove from this churning of India now in process; and the Brahmin would be wise to remember that legend while there is time.

IV

Thus far our guides; and a great deal of what they say is true. It would be difficult to libel the miserable being whom our Western system of education, manipulated by incompetent and often grossly dishonest Indians, has evolved. Every Englishman who has been in any position of responsibility in India knows how often he has had to interfere to save Indians from their own kin. The measures of self-government granted from time to time, municipal and parliamentary, have frequently been worked listlessly or—I am afraid it is impossible to avoid repetition of the word—dishonestly. The world's literature of abuse might be ransacked, and still the crown for utter irrelevance and reckless unfairness allowed to rest with the Indian extremist press. Nor is it (in my judgment) possible to exaggerate the services which Britain has rendered to India or the greatness of the individual contribution of many of her sons and daughters. I know that the heroisms of this Empire are innumerable, and that they throw about its daily traffic a splendour brighter by far than any which imagination flings about the thought of Cæsar's outposts on the Rhine or in Libya. These things will be seen and acknowledged one day, and no honest and competent mind will judge our rule hardly when its day has passed. It is no use looking for gratitude; the whole world is raw and bleeding, and we have all got memories that we had better forget.

But yet we must feel, when reading expositions of the Indian situation, that still there are things unexplained. This feeling is now reaching even the writers in our newspapers; it has been very noteworthy of late, the surprise with which people, who for years have been assuring us that

Indian "unrest" is a passing thing, engineered by a few self-seeking politicians, have discovered that the opposition to our rule has permeated all classes and is consolidating daily. Here is a fact, as disquieting as can be, which is explained by nothing that we have been told. Then, to take a comparatively small point: consider the alleged responsibility of the Brahmin for all discontent. But I take up a list of prominent Indian "extremists" and I run through the names. Certainly there are Brahmins there, just as in our own House of Lords there are Socialists and Moslems. But Gandhi is not a Brahmin; the Ali Brothers are not Brahmins; C. R. Das was not a Brahmin. Worse still, when I put aside the list of men who are simply "extremists," and come to the very small class of men who are really irreconcilables, the few who do *hate* Britain and the British—a class which, most emphatically, does not include a man like Gandhi—I do not most readily think of Brahmins. Going past the men whose differences with us could be, and one day will be, adjusted over a round table, leaving esteem and the beginnings of friendliness behind—the Indian Michael Collinses and Griffiths and Cosgraves—we come to countenances set hard in unforgiving, unforgetting warfare. Brahmins? Yes, some, of course; but the countenances that most swiftly rise to vision are not those of Brahmins.

I spoke of a "struggle" which is at its commencement. Yet may we not ask, Need there be a struggle at all? Having chosen in the case of South Africa the wisest and most magnanimous course of action that ever showed a nation's greatness—having at long last the promise of friendship with Ireland, and, through that finish of old enmity, with the United States—having long ago passed safely through the dangerous stages of our relations with Canada and Australia and New Zealand—can we not settle this latest of our great imperial problems also? Or, if there must be a struggle before there is peace, need it be embittered?

For my concern is not to try to show what we should do in India, but to try to help myself, puzzled and puzzling through many years of friendly intercourse with Indians, and any of my countrymen who care to listen, to understand what is at the root of the trouble. It seems to me that we are wasting time when we argue about the separation of judicial and executive functions in India, or the officering of the Indian army by Indians. These are the questions that politically minded Indians raise, meeting us within our own "universe of discourse." But there are many Indians who are not politically minded, whose conflict with us would continue, as things are at present, whatever administrative or military action we took. Nor do I feel that even politically minded Indians are doing more than meet us in adroit debate when they raise these questions. Greeks and Trojans fought over the body of Patroclus, because they had no choice but to spill their rancour round a symbol, the reality being withdrawn from the battle. But, had some unperceived band of marauding Greeks been able to effect a breach in the very walls of Troy, then in a moment dead Patroclus would have been left where he lay, while the armies raced for possession of the heart of the war, the unviolated city of Priam. So to-day, Indians and ourselves wrangle over dead Patroclus, over the Viceroy's powers of veto, over the rights of Indians to full Empire citizenship everywhere, over the grant of Dominion status. But were all these points conceded—even were we to withdraw every shred of control, and to leave India outside the Biitish connection—still, as matters are, the old bitterness would remain. Indians for centuries to come would crab every British achievement, would clack about our gross materialism, and would lie about us all over the world, as they do now. And the legend of our kindness and of Indian ingratitude would colour our school-books and our fiction, and be a subtle tinge and poison even in our scholarship, as it is now. Our publicists, when the pressure of more important affairs left them half an hour in which to explain the teeming sub-continent whose destinies we once controlled, would try to draw down the world's scorn upon a people so talkative and vain and inefficient and untruthful. We should both of us be like Bunyan's Pope, when he sat "in his cave's mouth, grinning at pilgrims as they go by, and biting his nails because he cannot come at them." So hate would continue from century to century. There would be something lacking of perfect chivalry even when Englishmen wrote of Kalidasa or Indians of Shakespeare.

VI

Apart from the things, whatever they are, that make for irreconcilability, there are, of course, many smaller things poisoning the Indian mind to-day. Many of these are not our fault, even though the extremist press would make everything our fault, as if we could bind the sweet influences of Pleiades or loose the bands of Orion. The average British official, whatever his faults, is keen on "doing his job"—to use the mystic phrase with which we cover up a multitude of merits as well as sins, excusing ourselves alike from the trouble of thinking and that of blowing our own trumpets. He is honestly out to do the best he can for the people under his charge; and whatever idleness or self-seeking there may be in the secretariats,[1] there is precious little in the district official, who is the eyes and hands of the Government—in short, *is* the Government, so far as it immediately concerns the people. But everything—it does not matter what it is—is twisted against the Government and its agents. If railways are built, it is that water may be banked up instead of draining away, so that mosquitoes and malaria may be increased; if railways are not built, it is because Government cares nothing for the needs of the district. This kind of thing is plausible only because the peasant is so helplessly in our hands, and is, moreover, so poor. "We are a half-starved nation," said Rabindranath Tagore to me once. "And our food has such little nourishment in it—just rice and vegetables." In our own islands it is clear that the struggle for existence is about to enter on a still more embittered course; it is extremely hard to make a living, as so many able ex-service men have found. Not all the bulls uttered against birth control can prevent people from more and more considering it as a necessity if we are to escape a barbaric and pitiless fight in a very few generations. India, too, is overpopulated, and lacks our means of aggrandising her own strained resources by effort outside herself. And a depressed and impoverished populace, however slow a soil to blossom with any sort of thought

[1] See Al. Carthill again.

whatever, will ultimately raise a more flaming crop of discontent than any other. This has been very well realised by Indian extremists, who have long been alive to the opportunities that flood and famine furnish for running relief work and propaganda conjointly, for scattering seeds of kindness and of rebellion from the same basket. Then there is the educational system, a source of cruel disillusionment and disappointment. But none of these things explain the existence of actual hatred of the British name. That this hatred exists—savage, set hatred—is certain; and the sooner we recognise it, and search for its reasons, the better. The discontent with our rule is growing universal, and there must be, first, widespread popular memories to account for that discontent being able to spread; and, secondly, blazing hatred at its heart, to have caused it to gather such rapid momentum.

Many Englishmen in India must have had my experience. They have been puzzling over the problem, honestly anxious to find out where the actual point of exasperation—no, more than exasperation, of severance—came, and to see if anything could be done. Then they have thought that they had found it—yes, it was here, see! They have pushed hard, only to find that they have gone through a curtain painted like a wall, to find the real wall, granite and immovable, behind.

CHAPTER II

THE MUTINY

I

IRRECONCILABILITY lies somewhere at the back of the mind; and the trouble is, one can never get there. That is why arguments between nations resemble, to use the old comparison, a battle between a shark and a tiger; keeping to diverse elements, they never come to grips, but ravage the invulnerable air and wave.

It is the harder to get at the back of the mind and remove the festering trouble there, when one side feels that conditions have been unfair and uequal. When one side has succeeded in imposing its version of events on the whole world, when one side controls history or the press, then underground bitterness becomes something too poisoned and ferocious for expression. The English, for all their power, have suffered too much from this kind of injustice to be unable to sympathise with Indians. Our dealings with Ireland, with South Africa, with the United States when they were our Colonies, bad as they sometimes were, were by no means so unrelievedly fiendish and unjustified as most of the world believes. The Irish, foiled of full expression in these islands, lied about us in America, lied luridly and efficiently; every orator knows how his style is helped by an enthusiastic audience in love with his subject-matter. The Boers lied about us on the Continent. The Americans, with less excuse, travestied — one does not use a stronger term about a business which to-day is receiving such handsome amends—our conduct before and during their Revolution and before the unnecessary war they forced on us when we were fighting for our existence against Napoleon. History is being generously rewritten to-day, to our great gain, and the world is beginning to see that the English are not only or always hypocrites or fiends. That we have endured so much gainsaying of men with, on the whole, so much dignity and quietness is now being reckoned to us for righteousness. But are there no other travesties of events in history-books? Now that American historians are so generously dispelling the clouds of old detraction of us, cannot we show the same magnanimity towards India? If we do, I am convinced that we shall get very close to one main fountain that is now sending forth a steady flood of poisoned waters, and we can cleanse its well of bitterness.

Indians are not historians; and they rarely

show any critical ability. Even their most useful books, books full of research and information, exasperate with their repetitions and diffuseness, and lose effect by their uncritical enthusiasms. Such solid highways to scholarly esteem and approval as indexes and bibliographies are almost unknown to them. So they are not likely to displace our account of our connection with India. They are not able to arrange their knowledge so as to gain that first essential towards a favourable judgment, a hearing. But if they *know* that our account of certain enormously important events is unfair—and how can they help but know, being so sensitively concerned with them?—their failure to set their knowledge forth will only deepen their resentment.

II

Why was there such an outcry in India against the *Oxford History of India*? The author,[1] though he wrote and probably thought coldly, was a man of fair and judicial mind and a sincere friend of India. His book shows an exhaustive research into authorities and a balanced proportion in treatment, for which Indians have yet to prove that they possess the necessary patience and detachment of mind. Yet Indians felt that these very qualities made his treatment of such

[1] Vincent Smith.

an episode as the Mutiny the more galling, his reticence being felt as deeply as the gross misrepresentation of other writers had been. A touch of fire and generosity, an anxiety not merely to set out events without palpable inaccuracy but also to correct old wrongs, would have made an exceedingly valuable book into a great one. But that fire and that generosity were lacking—and, since the book carried the *imprimatur* of Oxford, Indians felt that its icy exactitude would be an intolerable load oppressing them for many years to come.

The reader knows the impression he has gathered of Indians and of the British in India. Our histories and our novels have proceeded on certain clearly marked lines. There is the Indian, " half-devil and half-child," docile, patient, capable of a doglike devotion, given to mysticism and brooding contemplation, yet with all these good qualities liable to perversion into a treacherous seditionist or bloodthirsty fanatic ; there is the Englishman, silent, efficient, inflexibly just, dispensing to each his deserts. It is not strange that Indians should be restive under such a portrayal, or that even Kipling's magnificent work should be read with feelings of pain and humiliation. The interpretations of our history books, in the case of many events, they challenge. But in one case they rarely challenge them openly, because the deeds are too recent and too bitterly felt by both sides, and because the English interpretation of them is too firmly established for easy displacement. This case, unfortunately, is that of the one episode when we really were guilty of the cruellest injustice on the greatest scale. If we desire to eliminate bitterness from our controversy with India, we certainly have to readjust our ideas of this episode—the Mutiny. The Mutiny hardly stirred South India, and still does not deeply affect its thought. But there are many things, besides this fact, that have kept racial feeling and discontent from attaining in the South the intensity which marks them in the North; and it is in the North that the buried volcano is threatening to burst its way out, and it is from the North that seismic shocks are spreading all over India. Right at the back of the mind of many an Indian the Mutiny flits as he talks with an Englishman—an unavenged and unappeased ghost.

III

The pseudonymous author of *The Lost Dominion* —that pretentious and noxious book [1]—observes, in setting out the causes of the Mutiny, "All that is necessary is to remark that the Mutiny was in no sense a national revolt, except in Oudh, which

[1] A well-known Indian administrator demurs that this is unjust, and that the book is obviously "a very clever leg-pull." I think it may be.

was hardly part of the British dominions."[1] Oudh is so very large an exception that no writer who caıed that his statements should be worth setting down would have made a generalisation so qualified; and the generalisation is reduced to a bare fifty per cent. of truth if we add to Oudh Jhansi, and the Mahrattas who under Nana Sahib sought to restore the Peshwa's power, and the Musalmans who sought to restore the empire of Delhi. *The Oxford History of India* says:

"The rising, although primarily a military mutiny of the Bengal army, immediately provoked by the greased cartridges, was not confined to the troops. Discontent and unrest were widely prevalent among the civil population, and in several places the populace rose before the sepoys at those stations mutinied."[2]

Romesh Dutt says:

"It is beyond a doubt that political reasons helped a mere mutiny of soldiers to spread among large classes of the people in Northern and Central India, and converted it into a political insurrection. Lord Dalhousie's vast and rapid annexations had created an impression that the East India Company aimed at universal conquest; that they disregarded treaties and the laws of the country in order to compass their object. The minds of the people were unsettled; and leaders of the insurrection issued Proclamations dwelling on the bad-faith and the earth-hunger of the alien rulers."[3]

[1] P. 47. [2] P. 722. [3] *India in the Victorian Age*, p. 223.

An Indian who was in Delhi during our siege of it says:

"I will commence my narrative with the statement that, however the English may regard themselves, they are regarded by the natives as trespassers, and this feeling was intensified on the annexation of the province of Oude. . . . The English are familiar with the views of English writers on the causes of the mutiny of the Indian Army. These views differ in some respects from those held by natives." [1]

Disraeli, speaking on 27th July 1857, said that

"he was persuaded that the mutineers of the Bengal army were not so much the avengers of professional grievances as the exponents of general discontent. The old principle of our rule had been to respect nationality; but the Government of India of late years had alienated or alarmed almost every influential class." [2]

How far the movement was popular, a real war for independence, and how far merely the military mutiny it is always represented in our histories, is an unsolved problem. No other episode of first-class importance has been treated so uncritically or upon such one-sided and prejudged evidence.

The other main immediate cause, as everyone

[1] Nawab Main-ud-din Hassan Khan, in *Two Native Narratives of the Mutiny*, translated for and edited by Charles Theophilus Metcalfe, C.S.I., pp. 31, 32.

[2] *The Life of Benjamin Disraeli*, by George Earle Buckle, iv, 88.

knows, was the greased cartridges. A more perfect moral explosive could not have been found. Lecky says:

"The horrors of Cawnpore—which were due to a single man—soon took away from the British public all power of sanely judging the conflict, and a struggle in which no quarter was given was naturally marked by extreme savageness; but in looking back upon it, English writers must acknowledge with humiliation that, if mutiny is ever justifiable, no stronger justification could be given than that of the Sepoy troops."[1]

Lord Roberts quotes the letter of Anson, Commander-in-Chief when the Mutiny broke out, to Lord Canning:

"I am not so much surprised at their objections to the cartridges, having seen them. I had no idea they contained, or rather are smeared with such a quantity of grease, which looks exactly like fat. After ramming down the ball, the muzzle of the musket is covered with it";[2]

and states as his own opinion that

"incredible disregard of the soldiers' religious prejudices was displayed in the manufacture of these cartridges."[3]

When the use of this abhorrent mixture was forced upon them, it drove the troops out of their minds. Eighty-five men of the Third Cavalry

[1] *The Map of Life* (1901 edition), p. 104.
[2] *Forty-One Years in India*, i, 94.
[3] *Ibid.*, i, 431.

at Meerut refused to use them ; they were court-martialled and sentenced to ten years' penal servitude, a sentence reduced to five years in the case of eleven young troopers. This vindictive sentence was carried out in a way that outraged every sentiment of decency, on the 9th of May 1857.

"Under a guard of Rifles and Carabineers, the Eighty-five were then brought forward, clad in their regimental uniforms—soldiers still ; and then the sentence was read aloud, which was to convert soldiers into felons. Their accoutrements were taken from them, and their uniforms were stripped from their backs. Then the armourers and the smiths came forward with their shackles and their tools, and soon, in the presence of that great concourse of their old comrades, the Eighty-five stood, with the outward symbols of their dire disgrace fastened upon them. It was a piteous spectacle, and many there were moved with a great compassion, when they saw the despairing gestures of those wretched men, among whom were some of the very flower of the regiment—soldiers who had served the British Government in trying circumstances and in strange places, and who had never before wavered in their allegiance. Lifting up their hands and lifting up their voices, the prisoners implored the General to have mercy upon them, and not to consign them to so ignominious a doom. Then, seeing that there was no other hope, they turned to their comrades and reproached them for quietly suffering this disgrace to descend upon them. There was not a Sepoy present who did not feel the rising indignation in his throat. But in the presence of those loaded field-guns and those grooved rifles, and the glittering sabres of the Dragoons, there could not be a thought of striking. The prisoners were marched off to their cells, to be placed under the custody of a guard of their own countrymen." [1]

Lord Canning called the "consigning the eighty-five prisoners, after such a ceremony, to the gaol, with no other than a native guard over them," "a folly that is inconceivable"; [2] and of the whole proceedings he observed, at a later date, when replying to the clamour for executions and yet more executions,

> "there is no ground for supposing that the careful moderation exhibited by the Government at the outburst of the Mutiny encouraged its spread. On the contrary, the first great act of rebellion was the immediate result of a severe sentence carried out, with every degrading accessory, at Meerut." [3]

Next day,

> "the cavalry and two infantry regiments broke open the jail, released their comrades, burnt the officers' houses, murdered every European on whom they could lay hands, and hurried off to Delhi. The begin-

[1] Kaye, *History of the Sepoy War* (9th edition, 1880), Book IV, Chapter ii.

[2] *Letter to Mr Vernon Smith*, 5th June 1857. See also Roberts, *Forty-One Years in India* (25th edition, 1897), i, 82.

[3] *Earl Canning*, by Sir Henry Cunningham ("Rulers of India" series).

ning of the Mutiny is usually counted from that day, 10th May."[1]

At Delhi their arrival was followed by a brutal massacre of Europeans, men, women, and children; and another of the world's great servile revolts was in full blast, with all its accompaniments of sickening terror and cruelty.

IV

For in the world's history the uprisings of slaves against their masters stand out, a record of suffering and devilish cruelty on both sides. There is no quarter in such wars, never has been. Terrorism wars with terrorism, till the stronger side issues its bulletin to the world. Unrest among the slaves of Jamaica in the eighteenth century was punished by burnings alive and breakings on the wheel; their descendants, in Governor Eyre's time (1865), were crushed by wholesale use of whip and gallows. In Demerara, in 1824,

> "Twenty-three were put to death out of hand by the sole order of Colonel Leahy, and a Court-Martial hanged many more. Martial Law continued for five calendar months, nearly two hundred prisoners were tried, and within a month forty-seven of them were hanged in small batches. Many of them were hung in chains on the public roads, and the decapitated heads of others

[1] *Oxford History of India*, p. 715.

were exposed upon poles. The cruellest floggings were ordered, the number of lashes varying from 200 to 1000 each."[1]

In the United States to-day, not only savage lust or murder, but sometimes small or unproven offences on the part of negroes, are visited every year by lynching, often in the form of burning at the stake.[2]

But amid servile discontents military revolts have had a ghastly pre-eminence, for the simple reason that both sides have been armed and capable of cruelties which led to reprisal. The mutiny of Carthaginian mercenaries, between the first two Punic wars, was crushed by many thousands of crucifixions. The gladiators' rising under Spartacus was ended in the same way, when Pompey erected six thousand crosses on the highroad from Rome to Ostia. The Indian Mutiny, in the cautious language of the *Oxford History*, was

"marked by many deeds of horror, by infinite suffering, and not a few acts on both sides which it is painful to recall";[3]

and in the words of a less restrained writer, who certainly does not exaggerate,

"the contest seemed to lie between two savage races, capable of no thought but that, regardless of all justice

[1] *Smith of Demerara*, by David Chamberlin, p. 73.
[2] The practice is decreasing, happily.
[3] P. 723.

or mercy, their enemies should be exterminated. Deeds of cruelty on one side and on the other were perpetrated, over which it is necessary to draw a veil." [1]

But in English histories that veil, though drawn over the excesses of our own infuriated forces, has not been drawn over those of the infuriated mutineers. It is necessary that we should look, once, clearly and finally, at the side which has been hidden from ourselves; then we shall understand in part what madness is working subtly in the Indian mind to-day. One example of the official executions will suffice, that of 10th June 1857, at Peshawar. A hundred and twenty prisoners had been taken in an abortive rising.

"It was not to be doubted that the time had come when the severity of the hour would be the humanity of all time. But these rebels, though taken fighting against their masters, had not shed the blood of their officers, and there were some amongst them who, in the tumult of the hour, had been carried away by the multitude without any guilty intent. The voice of mercy, therefore, was lifted up. 'I must say a few words for some of the Fifty-fifth prisoners,' wrote Nicholson to Edwardes. 'The officers of that regi-

[1] Frank Bright, *History of England, Period IV*, p. 328 (quoted by Romesh Dutt, *India in the Victorian Age*).

ment all concur in stating that the Sikhs were on their side to the last. I would, therefore, temper stern justice with mercy, and spare the Sikhs and young recruits. Blow away all the rest by all means, but spare boys scarcely out of their childhood, and men who were really loyal and respectful up to the moment when they allowed themselves to be carried away in a panic by the mass.' And Sir John Lawrence wrote: '. . . . they were taken fighting against us, and so far deserve little mercy. But, on full reflection, I would not put them all to death. I do not think we should be justified in the eyes of the Almighty in doing so. A hundred and twenty men are a large number to put to death. Our object is to make an example to terrify others. I think this object would be effectively gained by destroying from a quarter to a third of them. I would select all those against whom anything bad can be shown—such as general bad character, turbulence, prominence in disaffection or in the fight, disrespectful demeanour to their officers during the few days before the 26th, and the like. If these did not make up the required number, I would then add to them the oldest soldiers. All these should be shot or blown away from guns, as may be most expedient. The rest I would divide into batches: some to be imprisoned ten years, some seven, some five, some three.' "[1]

Lawrence's letter is a voice out of a world which we have left for ever; its piety is an incredible thing to-day. There is even a grotesque echo of the Prayer Book in the last sentence but one. But

[1] Kaye, Book VI, Chapter iv.

this piety is very marked in the records of the Mutiny. Lieutenant Roberts, later Lord Roberts of Kandahar, writing to his mother the day after the executions at Peshawar, which we have just seen Lawrence discussing, remarks cheerily:

"Well, the troops assembled at Jhelum, and we have come along this far, doing a little business on the road such as disarming Regiments and executing mutineers. The death that seems to have the most effect is being blown from a gun. It is rather a horrible sight, but in these times we cannot be particular. Drum Head Courts-Martial are the order of the day in every station." [1]

The purpose of this "business," Roberts says, is to

"show these rascally Musalmans that, with God's help, Englishmen will still be masters of India"; [2]

and in a letter to his sister, in December, he is very confident that the joint efforts of our troops and their great Ally are nearing a happy issue:

"by the middle of February the rebels will be, please God, nearly exterminated." [3]

It is hard to understand why Victorian theologians, with this great mass of Mutiny literature contemporary with them and hall-marked with

[1] *Letters Written During the Indian Mutiny*, 11th June 1857.
[2] *Ibid.*, Letter written 31st December 1857.
[3] *Ibid.*, Letter written 28th December 1857.

general approval, should have been troubled by the alleged blood-thirstiness of the Old Testament. The Book of Joshua, by comparison, is a gentle and chivalrous record. One looks back wistfully to the time of our grandfathers. They, surely, were untroubled by the things which make it so hard for us to be convinced that Love rules and orders the world. The Great War should have been fought in their time; instead of disillusionment, it would have brought a mighty refreshing of faith.

It was decided that forty was the number of executions which would appear adequate in the eyes of Divine Justice; and forty men were therefore blown to pieces on 10th June, in as public and dreadful a manner as possible.

> "It is a significant fact that neither Sir Herbert Edwardes, in his Official Peshawur Report, nor Sir Sydney Cotton in his published Narrative, says one word about this punishment-parade. And what these brave men, being eye-witnesses of the horror, shrunk from describing, I may well abstain from dwelling on in detail. There is no lack, however, of particulars, all ghastly and some grotesque, in the cotemporary letters before me." [1]

As Kaye indicates, few who witnessed or heard this savage punishment practised the reticence of Edwardes and Cotton. Before the Mutiny had

[1] Kaye, Book VI, Chapter iv.

run many weeks of its course our people had so supped full of this particular horror that they had ceased to be squeamish in describing it. We may take our picture from a lady, a clergyman's widow:

"Many prisoners were hanged after the battle, and as it was discovered they did not care for hanging, four were tried and sentenced to be blown from guns; accordingly one day we were startled by hearing a gun go off, with an indescribably horrid muffled sound. . . . An officer told us it was a most sickening sight. . . . One gun was overcharged, and the poor wretch was literally blown into atoms, the lookers-on being covered with blood and fragments of flesh: the head of one poor wretch fell upon a bystander and hurt him."[1]

VI

Execution by blowing from guns was a punishment that the East India Company inherited[2] from the old Mogul Empire, whose successor and continuation it was. It was by no means the worst thing it took over. If there is one torture of the past which to-day stirs deeper horror than any other it is impalation; it is the mental realisation of this anguish that makes many people feel that *Hassan* is too painful to see or even to

[1] Mrs Coopland, *A Lady's Escape from Gwalior*, p. 233.

[2] It was used also by Lally, the Frenchman, and by the Mahrattas.

read. Yet a Bengal file contains a letter from an English officer, writing in the last years of the eighteenth century, which asks "how much longer are we to be outraged by the sight of writhing humanity on stakes?" Blowing from guns inflicted no kind of torture except—a very great reservation—mental. Yet by our use of it we placed ourselves beside that Mogul Empire which we despise; and the exhibition in Europe of pictures [1] of Russians hanging Polish prisoners and of the British blowing Indian prisoners to pieces conveyed the same impression of barbarous brutal empire, alike in Muscovite and Anglo-Saxon. And barbarous it certainly was. We can well believe that the "rude people of the border"—to whom torture and death were pleasing spectacles—

> "had no longer any misgivings with respect to the superiority of a race that could do such great things, calmly and coolly, and with all the formality of an inspection-parade." [2]

Earlier than this, Nicholson—the "Nikkul Seyn" who has been the hero-god of our boyhood's dreams, who more than any other man has been the prototype of the "strong, silent, God's Englishman" of our fiction—wrote to Edwardes:

> "Let us propose a Bill for the flaying alive, impalement, or burning of the murderers of the women and

[1] By Vereshchagin.

[2] Kaye, Book VI, Chapter iv.

children at Delhi. The idea of simply hanging the perpetrators of such atrocities is maddening. I wish that I were in that part of the world, that if necessary I might take the law into my own hands."[1]

A little later he brings—*more Anglorum*—religion into the argument:

"As regards torturing the murderers of the women and children: If it be right otherwise, I do not think we should refrain from it, because it is a Native custom. We are told in the Bible that stripes shall be meted out according to faults, and if hanging is sufficient punishment for such wretches, it is too severe for ordinary mutineers. If I had them in my power to-day, and knew that I were to die to-morrow, I would inflict the most excruciating tortures I could think of on them with a perfectly easy conscience."[1]

But Nicholson's letters are wrung from an anguished mind. They are infinitely less revolting than the nauseating stuff which came, we are told, from "one of the purest hearts and one of the soundest heads in all our Christian community." It was addressed to Henry Tucker, Commissioner of Benares:

"I fear in your case your natural tenderness. But, consider that we have to crucify these affections as well as our lusts. The magistrate bears not the sword in vain. The Word of God gives no authority to the modern tenderness for human life which would save

[1] Quoted by Kaye, Book VI, Chapter i.

even the murderer. . . . It is necessary in all Eastern lands to establish a fear and awe of the Government. Then, and not till then, are its benefits appreciated."[1]

Emerson, writing in 1856, observed:

"The doctrine of the Old Testament is the religion of England. The first leaf of the New Testament it does not open."[2]

Cooper, Deputy-Commissioner of Amritsar, writing during these first months of the Mutiny, tells us that the principle on which the Punjab officers acted—and Cooper most emphatically did so himself—was to get your atrocity in first, and make it so terrible that the other side would be too cowed to think of perpetrating any answering atrocity:

"Even in the Punjab . . . where the people are as yet on the whole loyal, the execution, by order of Mr Montgomery, of a subahdar of a Sikh battalion, of the resaldar of the mounted police, and of the gaol darogah, for *having failed in their duty to the State*,[3] was necessary, to show publicly in the eyes of all men, that, at all events, the Punjab authorities adhered to the policy of overawing, *by a prompt and stern initiative*[4] (the only way to strike terror into its semi-barbarous people), and to the last would brook nothing short of absolute,

[1] Quoted by Kaye, Book VI, Chapter i.

[2] *English Traits, XIII, Religion.*

[3] Cooper's italics.

[4] My italics.

active, and positive loyalty. Government could not condescend to exist upon the moral sufferance of its subjects." [1]

The tortures which Nicholson advocated were not long in forthcoming. Mowbray Thomson [2] told Sir Henry Cotton of the fate of some prisoners he once took:

"Late in the evening a Sikh orderly came to his tent, and, saluting, said: 'I think, sir, you would like to see what we have done to the prisoners.' Suspecting the worst, he sprang up and rushed to the guard-room, and there witnessed the spectacle of these wretched Mohammedans at their last gasp, tied to the ground stripped of their clothing, and deeply branded over every part of their bodies from head to foot with red-hot coppers. With his own hand he put an end to their agony by blowing out their brains. 'Good God!' said I, when I heard the story, 'and what happened?' 'Nothing,' was the reply." [3]

Why should anything have happened? Eastern minds have long memories. The English memory is more easygoing and brief than any other national memory, which is why we are so amazed when we find that other people remember hangings or shootings that are quite fifty years old; and these Sikhs remembered the ferocious tortures

[1] *The Crisis in the Punjab*, pp. 151, 152.
[2] One of the very few survivors of Cawnpore.
[3] Cotton, *Indian and Home Memories*, p. 143.

with which their ancestors had been executed by the Mogul Empire a hundred and fifty years before. That wheel came full circle in the Mutiny, when the Sikhs against Delhi were our most savage and joyous auxiliaries.

An eye-witness tells how Sikhs and Europeans together, after repeatedly bayoneting a wounded prisoner in the face, burnt him alive over a slow fire:

> "... the horrible smell of his burning flesh as it cracked and blackened in the flames, rising up and poisoning the air—so in this nineteenth century, with its boasted civilisation and humanity, a human being should lie roasting and consuming to death, while Englishmen and Sikhs gathered in little knots around, looked calmly on. No one will deny, I think, that this man, at least, adequately expiated, by his frightful and cruel death, any crimes of which he may have been guilty." [1]

Russell, the *Times* war correspondent, has an account of the same incident, and adds: "I saw the charred bones, some days after, on the plain." [2]

The record of my country is cleaner from such deeds of deliberate cruelty than the record of any other country on the globe. The story of mankind is a melancholy one; but we have at least

[1] Lieut. Majendie, *Up among the Pandies*, p. 187. Crimes, of course, is a *façon de parler*. It was taken for granted that every sepoy had murdered women and children.

[2] *My Diary in India in the Year* 1858–9, i, 301, 302.

the right to claim that, though often ruthless, we have rarely been fiends. This incident is exceptional in our annals; but the whole Mutiny episode was exceptional. The brave Irishman who did more than anyone else to introduce into it the first faint recognitions of the claims of humanity,[1] wrote:

> "All these kinds of vindictive, unchristian, Indian torture, such as sewing Mohammedans in pig-skins, smearing them with pork-fat before execution, and burning their bodies, and forcing Hindoos to defile themselves, are disgraceful, and ultimately recoil on ourselves. They are spiritual and mental tortures to which we have no right to resort, and which we dare not perpetrate in the face of Europe."[2]

I know nothing more illustrative of the uncritical and incurious character of my people's minds than the way we have accepted the version of the Mutiny that was imposed upon us when it finished. The facts are better known almost everywhere else; this is part of the reason why Europe has been so unimpressed by our quite genuine anxiety to save Armenians or Poles from torture and extermination.

[1] "Delane,"—editor of the *Times*—"attributed the cessation of indiscriminate executions to Russell's first letter from Cawnpore," *Dictionary of National Biography*, article on Russell.

[2] Russell, *Diary*, ii, 43 (May 1858).

"Foreign nations are watching us as closely as they can; but there is a long space of land and sea to cross. . . . A French general, in a letter to Sir Colin, expressed his regret at certain violences attributed to some of our officers in cold blood . . . but he should know that here there is no cold blood at the sight of a rebel."[1]

VII

But was nothing done to save our character as a civilised and Christian nation? Yes, a great deal was; and, ineffective as it was, the protest stood to our honour and stands to-day. In India detailed instructions drawn up on 31st July 1857 by the Governor-General-in-Council forbade the indiscriminate burning of villages and prohibited civilians from punishing any unarmed man as a mere deserter. Several commissions with power of life and death were withdrawn from civilians who had used them ferociously. On 28th August Mr John Grant was sent to the Central Provinces as Lieutenant-Governor to check the indiscriminate hangings at Allahabad and other places. There was a great outcry against "anti-hangman Grant" and "Clemency Canning." In August, British troops returning from a village-burning expedition shot and bayoneted a number of loyal sepoys; this the *Times*[2] called "wild justice,"

[1] Russell, i, 221, 222.
[2] 24th October 1857 (Montgomery Martin).

but Outram termed it "cold-blooded murder." And in September Outram wrote to Grant:

> "It is high time to show we do not propose to wage war to the knife and to extermination against all Hindoos, or against all sepoys because they are sepoys."

A month later, the *Times*[1] still held that there were

> "few persons who would not think a simple extermination of the sepoys on the field of battle rather a tame conclusion of the affair."

But, a few months later,[2] even the *Times* thought that the efforts to control the flood of massacre had been not unwise:

> "The indiscriminate slaughter of the sepoys might, perhaps, have led to the revolt of the Bombay and Madras armies."

It might, indeed. There can be no question that very many sepoys were terrified, first into desertion or mutiny and then into a desperate resistance that cost us dearly. There never was any quarter shown. A subaltern wrote home to a sister:

> "You must not think, darling Harriet, that I pity the sepoys or blackguards who are rebelling against us.

[1] 21st October 1857 (Montgomery Martin).
[2] 6th February 1858 (Montgomery Martin).

On the contrary, few are more unrelenting than I am. When a prisoner is brought in, I am the first to call out to have him hanged."[1]

Cooper tells us:

"Short shrift awaited all captures. The motto of General Nicholson for mutineers was *à la lanterne*."[2]

A clergyman's widow observes triumphantly:

"They took a great many prisoners, and made them clean out the church;[3] but as it was contrary to their 'caste,' they were obliged to do it at the point of the bayonet: some did it with alacrity, thinking they would be spared hanging; but they were mistaken, for they were all hung."[4]

Majendie, again:

"I spent that night on picket at the Musjid above mentioned, much of our time being passed in shooting or hanging prisoners taken during the day. . . . Many

[1] Roberts, Letter dated 26th February 1858. And his family saw fit to allow the publication of the letters in the year 1923, not regarding—or else despising—the reverence with which many Indians remember his name. They surely cannot have supposed that the extreme moderation with which the Mutiny is described and discussed—at great length—in his own *Forty-One Years in India*, was not deliberate.

[2] *The Crisis in the Punjab*, p. 149.

[3] Of Fatehpur Sikri.

[4] *A Lady's Escape from Gwalior*, p. 243. It is fair to remember that her husband had been murdered.

a poor wretch breathed his last at this spot, dying, for the most part, with a calmness and courage worthy of a better cause." [1]

An officer before Delhi wrote that the enemy

"have not attempted to capitulate, because they know that nothing but death will satisfy English soldiers. . . . Nought else shall they have at our hands." [2]

These were General Neill's instructions to Major Renaud, when he was hurrying with an advance-guard to the relief of Cawnpore :

"Certain guilty villages were marked out for destruction, and all the men inhabiting them were to be slaughtered. All sepoys of mutinous regiments not giving a good account of themselves were to be hanged. The town of Futtehpore, which had revolted, was to be attacked, and the Pathan quarters destroyed with all their inhabitants. 'All heads of insurgents, particularly at Futtehpore, to be hanged.' If the Deputy-Collector is taken, hang him, and have his head cut off and stuck up on one of the principal (Mahomedan) buildings of the town." [3]

[1] P. 205.

[2] *Times*, 24th October 1857 (Montgomery Martin). Similarly, Greathed (*Letters*, pp. 165, 166): "A Moulvee had the courage to tell them . . . that as they could not hope for victory they had better endeavour to get terms. But they have not even that hope to trust to, and nothing but death stares them in the face."

[3] Kaye, Book V, Chapter ii.

In 1858, the Begam of Oudh, in a proclamation, said with despairing dignity:

> "No one has ever seen in a dream that the English forgave an offence."[1]

At length, not only Canning but John Lawrence also tried to check the indiscriminate butchery; and Disraeli from the first spoke out courageously. When the tempest of passion was at its height, he spoke thus—not a protest against the action of a foreign nation, but against that of his own maddened people:

> "The horrors of war need no stimulant. The horrors of a war carried on as the war in India is at present especially need no stimulant. I am persuaded that our soldiers and our sailors will exact a retribution which it may perhaps be too terrible to pause upon. But I do without the slightest hesitation declare my humble disapprobation of persons in high authority announcing that upon the standards of England 'vengeance,' and not 'justice,' should be inscribed. . . . I for one protest against taking Nana Sahib as a model for the conduct of the British soldier. I protest against meeting atrocities by atrocities. I have heard things said and seen things written of late which would make me almost suppose that the religious opinions of the people of England had undergone some sudden change, and that,

[1] Montgomery Martin, *Rise and Progress of the Indian Mutiny*, Chapter xxvi.

instead of bowing before the name of Jesus, we were preparing to revive the worship of Moloch." [1]

Of the temper of the European community in India Lord Canning wrote to Queen Victoria :

"There is a rabid and indiscriminate vindictiveness abroad, even among many who ought to set a better example, which it is impossible to contemplate without a feeling of shame for one's countrymen. . . . Not one man in ten seems to think that the hanging and shooting of 40,000 or 50,000 men can be otherwise than practicable and right."

The Queen replied :

"Lord Canning will easily believe how entirely the Queen shares his feelings of sorrow and indignation at the unchristian spirit shown also to a great extent here by the public towards India in general." [2]

Unfortunately, Canning's sentiments were stronger than his actions. Sir George Campbell, who speaks of "the exuberant severity of the Courts-Martial and Special Commissioners" and observes :

[1] *Life*, by Buckle, iv, 98, 99 (Speech at Newport Pagnell, 30th September 1857).

[2] Possibly, when Disraeli persuaded Victoria in 1876 to assume the title of Empress of India, his motives had in them something nobler and more humane than anyone has ever guessed, and Mr Lytton Strachey's treatment of his action (*Queen Victoria*, pp. 262, 263) may be as unjust as it is striking.

"I have often heard of 'martial law,' and have known a good many occasions on which energetic people demanded 'martial law,' but to this day I have never been able to make out what it means, unless it be a general leave to any military person to kill anyone, take any property, or do anything else he pleases. That is, I think, what is generally understood, though not exactly expressed,"[1]

says:

"When Lord Canning's Government passed that Act of 6th June 1857, and proclaimed Martial Law in certain provinces, they were bound to exercise the strictest executive control over the manner in which such terrible engines were used. And while giving Lord Canning every honour for the principles of clemency which he inculcated, I cannot forgive him the extreme administrative inefficiency which allowed those principles to be set at naught in practice, and blood to be shed in a most reckless manner. . . . There was very little of the formalities of military law in what was done."

Sir George Campbell raises another matter, our indiscriminate butchery of all the people in arms against us, whether mutinous sepoys or the inhabitants of Oudh:

"though the sepoys were possessed by a kind of madness, still they were men who, having eaten our salt, had turned on us in the most savage manner;

[1] *Memoirs of My Indian Career*, i, 232.

whereas, when our power was completely swept away, and there was nothing but anarchy, we could hardly expect all our native subjects to remain devoted to us as if they had been our own countrymen, or attribute much moral guilt to those who thought our day was past and set up for themselves. The wonder, I think, is that so few did so. Wherever the sepoys broke out, as a rule they murdered all the Europeans they came across. It was the exception when they did not do so. On the other hand, among the civil population our fugitives were generally spared and often assisted; it was quite the exception when they were murdered."[1]

The same thing had occurred to a much simpler mind than Campbell's:

"this to my mind is one of the most melancholy features of the war, that so many comparatively innocent beings should have suffered, as many have done, and that so little distinction should have been made between the cowardly mutineer, red-handed with the slaughter of women and children, and the Oude villager, or 'budmash,' who, whatever other acts of injustice and rapine he may have committed, and whatever his private character, cannot be said to have been guilty of rebellion, nor had done any of these deeds, but simply taken advantage of a great revolt to strike a blow for his country, which we had taken from him, and who was fighting—whether wisely or not is another question—with at least a show of right upon his side, and in a cause which was not wholly vile . . . it would have been

[1] *Memoirs of My Indian Career*, i, 233.

more satisfactory if for the people of Oude—sepoys excepted—there had been some mercy and quarter." [1]

Russell summarises this question thus:

"Either it was a military mutiny, or it was a rebellion more or less favoured by the people when once the soldiery broke into insurrection. If it was a pure military insurrection, it is most unjust to punish the country people and citizens by fine and hanging for complicity in acts with which they of their own accord had nothing to do; it is also impolitic to inflict chastisement upon them for not actively resisting armed men, drilled and disciplined by ourselves, and masters for the time of the whole country. We cannot punish sympathies: the attempt is sure to quicken animosities and provoke national, deep-rooted antipathy. Let us slay the sepoys in the field, let us destroy our enemies in battle, let us take the life of those murderous traitors who cruelly slew their officers, and hacked to pieces in cold blood women and children. But to punish 'districts' because evil deeds were committed therein, or because bodies of the enemy selected them to encamp and live in, is as unjust as it is unwise. . . . The mutinies have produced too much hatred and ill-feeling between the two races to render any mere change of

[1] Majendie, p. 195. Majendie's thought and style are rambling —"comparatively innocent beings" means Indians who were executed because they were Indians; and, of course, only a very small proportion of sepoys had murdered women and children. And the Oudh "budmash" was *méchant* only in the sense that, like the cat, when attacked he defended himself. But his shortcomings as thinker and writer make Majendie an excellent representative of the ordinary officer.

the name of the rulers a remedy for the evils which affect India; and however desirable it might have been to introduce that change, I do not think it was cheaply purchased at the price of much innocent blood, and by the growth of bitter hostility between the natives and the members of the race to which their rulers belong. Many years must elapse ere the evil passions excited by these disturbances expire; *perhaps confidence will never be restored.*"[1]

VIII

Frederick Cooper, Deputy-Commissioner of Amritsar, wrote a book[2] about the exploit which, he believed, would make him eternally famous. That exploit was announced by the Foreign Office in London[3] thus:

> "The 26th N.I. mutinied at Lahore on the 30th of July, and murdered the commanding officer, Major Spencer; but the mutineers were totally destroyed."

On 13th May the 3800 Indian troops at Lahore were disarmed as a precautionary measure. For nearly three months Sikhs and about 400 Europeans watched them night and day. During a violent dust-storm on 30th July there was observed some commotion among them, which British officers afterwards said was panic at the storm.

[1] *Diary*, ii, 259. His own italics.

[2] *The Crisis in the Punjab*. My quotations are from Cooper's own account.

[3] 28th September 1857.

"Whether there had been any preconcerted scheme among the disarmed regiments for a general attempt to escape from their unpleasant position is not known . . . a fanatic, named Prakash Sing, rushed out of his hut, brandishing a sword, and bawling out to his comrades to rise and kill the Feringhees."

He cut down the Major, whereupon the 26th Native Infantry fled under cover of the storm, the few who remained being killed in a furious cannonade which the Sikhs and Europeans put down on their lines. They tried to cross the Ravi next day, but were opposed by some police. Mr Cooper pursued them from Amritsar, and found this situation:

"The villagers were assembled on the bank, flushed with their easy triumph over the mutineers, of whom some 150 had been shot, mobbed backwards into the river, and drowned inevitably; too weakened and famished as they must have been after their forty miles' flight to battle with the flood. The main body had fled upwards, and swam over on pieces of wood, or floated to an island about a mile off from the shore, where they might be descried crouching like a brood of wild fowl. It remained to capture this body, and having done so, to execute condign punishment at once."

But Mr Cooper was confronted with the difficulty of the man who had to transport across a river a fox, a goose, and a sack of corn. He dare not leave fox and goose or goose and corn together, or either fox or goose alone. He explained the fable to his Sikhs, and the grim practical joke he intended to play on the sepoys, and the Sikhs, he tells us, were immensely diverted with his merry humour. However, everything went well; and his mind, being both pious and poetical, drank in the rich beauty and fitness of the whole scene, recording them afterwards:

"Everything natural, artificial, and accidental favoured the attempt and combined to secure the fate of the mutineers. . . . At any moment, had they made an attempt to escape, a bloody struggle must have ensued. But Providence ordered otherwise, and nothing on the side of the pursuing party seemed to go wrong. . . . The sun was setting in golden splendour; and as the doomed men, with joined palms,[1] crowded down to the shore on the approach of the boats,[2] one side of which bristled with about sixty muskets, besides sundry revolvers and pistols—their long shadows were flung far athwart the gleaming waters. In utter despair, forty or fifty dashed into the stream; and the sowars being on the point of taking pot-shots at the heads of the swimmers, orders were given not to fire."

The sepoys, being silly folk, jumped to the conclusion that Mr Cooper intended to give them a trial:

"They evidently were possessed of a sudden and insane idea that they were going to be tried by court-

[1] Begging for mercy.

[2] He sent off two boats to the island.

martial, after some luxurious refreshment. In consequence of which, thirty-six stalwart sepoys submitted to be bound by a single man, and stocked like slaves into a hold into one of the two boats emptied for the purpose."

By midnight he had 282 prisoners in a bastion at the police-station. There were also " numbers of camp-followers, who were left to be taken care of by the villagers." They pass out of the story, and no inquiry was ever made as to what happened to them. Rain fell, causing the execution to be deferred, but at the same time tinging the scene with a melancholy beauty that was not lost upon Mr Cooper's sensitive and religious mind :

" The gracious moon, which came out through the clouds and reflected herself in myriad pools and streams, as if to light the prisoners to their fate."

Next morning a party of Sikhs arrived with a large supply of rope ; the rope was not used, as trees were scarce, but the Sikhs enabled Mr Cooper to get rid of his Musalman troopers, whose loyalty, he feared, might not stand the strain of what he intended to do.

" The 1st of August was the anniversary of the great Mohammedan sacrificial festival of the Bukra Eed. A capital excuse was thus afforded to permit the Hindoostanee Mussulman horsemen to return to celebrate it at Umritsir ; while the single Christian, unembarrassed by their presence, and aided by the faithful Seiks, might perform a ceremonial sacrifice of a different nature. . . . As fortune would have it, again favouring audacity, a deep dry well was discovered within one hundred yards of the police-station, and its presence furnished a convenient solution as to the one remaining difficulty which was of sanitary consideration—the disposal of the corpses of the dishonoured soldiers."

The prisoners were pinioned, tied together, and brought out thus, in batches of ten, to be shot. They were filled with astonishment and rage when they learned their fate.

"About 150 having been thus executed, one of the executioners swooned away (he was the oldest of the firing-party), and a little respite was allowed. Then proceeding, the number had arrived at 237; when the district officer was informed that the remainder refused to come out of the bastion, where they had been imprisoned temporarily, a few hours before. . . . The doors were opened, and, behold! Unconsciously the tragedy of Holwell's Black Hole had been re-enacted. . . . Forty-five bodies, dead from fright, exhaustion, fatigue, heat, and partial suffocation, were dragged into light."

These, dead and dying, along with their murdered comrades, were thrown by the village sweepers into the well. Cooper continues:

"The above account, written by the principal actor in the scene himself, might read strangely at home: a single Anglo-Saxon, supported by a section of Asiatics, undertaking so tremendous responsibility, and coldly presiding over so memorable an execution, without the excitement of battle, or a sense of individual injury, to imbue the proceedings with the faintest hue of vindictiveness. The Governors of the Punjab are of the true English stamp and mould, and knew that England expected every man to do his duty, and that duty done, thanks them warmly for doing it."

Cooper's *Preface* strikes the same note—his book, he says, has been written to show how the Punjab is governed, and also

"that wisdom and that heroism are still but mere dross before the manifest and wondrous interposition of Almighty God in the cause of Christianity."

His book ends:

"To those fond of reading signs, we would point to the solitary golden cross still gleaming aloft on the summit of the Christian church in Delhi, whole and untouched; though the ball on which it rests is riddled with shots deliberately fired by the infidel populace. The cross symbolically triumphant over a shattered globe!"

It is true that later,

"For this splendid assumption of responsibility Cooper was assailed, as other men of his mettle, both in the East and the West Indies, have been, by the hysterical cries of ignorant humanitarians"; [1]

[1] T. R. E. Holmes, *The Indian Mutiny*, 4th edition, p. 353. Holmes's book, according to the *Oxford History of India*, is "the best book on the subject for most readers" (p. 731).

true, also, that the first claps of enthusiastic approval were succeeded by questioning and disgust, even in India, which at last so prevailed that his action is passed over in silence by our histories. But at the time the approbation for which he confidently looked was forthcoming. John Lawrence wrote:

"LAHORE, *2nd August*, 1857.

"MY DEAR COOPER,—I congratulate you on your success against the 26th N.I. You and your police acted with much energy and spirit, and deserve well of the State. I trust the fate of these sepoys will operate as a warning to others. Every effort should be exerted to glean up all who are yet at large."

Robert Montgomery, who succeeded Lawrence as Lieutenant-Governor of the Punjab, wrote:

"*Sunday*: 9 a.m.

"MY DEAR COOPER,—All honour for what you have done; and right well you did it. There was no hesitation, or delay, or drawing back. It will be a feather in your cap as long as you live. . . . The other three regiments here were very shaky yesterday; but I hardly think they will now go. I wish they would, as they are a nuisance; and not a man would escape if they do."

Montgomery[1] was a leading advocate of the propagation of Christianity in India. I do not

[1] "His benevolence was recognised in the service in India by the nickname of 'Pickwick,'" *Dictionary of National Biography*.

think it would be possible to comment on his letter adequately. After the Mutiny he wrote to Lawrence:

"It was not policy, or soldiers, or officers, that saved the Indian Empire to England, and saved England to India. The Lord our God, He it was."[1]

A short time after Cooper's exploit he wrote to Hodson, congratulating him on a deed which has found hardly any defenders, even among the writers of Mutiny memoirs:

"MY DEAR HODSON,—All honour to you (and to your 'Horse') for catching the king and slaying his sons. I hope you will bag many more!

"In haste, ever yours,

"R. MONTGOMERY."

But the story of Cooper's action is not quite finished. There was one sepoy so severely wounded that he could not walk to the place of execution. He was reprieved for Queen's evidence by "Pickwick" Montgomery's advice:

"Get out of the wounded man all you can, and send him to Lahore, that he may himself proclaim what has been done. The people will not otherwise believe it. . . . There will be some stragglers: have them all picked up; and any you get, send us now. You have had slaughter enough. We want a few for the troops here, and also for evidence."[2]

[1] *Lord Lawrence* ("Rulers of India" series), p. 114.

[2] Montgomery Martin, Chapter xxii.

So the wounded prisoner and another forty-one who were "gleaned" from the surrounding country were sent to Lahore, where they were all blown to pieces. In Cooper's words, "the 26th were both accounted for and disposed of." As for his own executions,

"'within forty-eight hours of the date of the crime, there fell by the law nearly 500 men.' What crime? what law? the reader may ask, demanded the extermination of a helpless multitude, described by the very best authority as unarmed and panic-stricken, famishing with hunger, and exhausted with fatigue?"[1]

Greathed remarks:

"the sacrifice of five hundred villanous lives for the murder of two English is a retribution that will be remembered."[2]

Yes, it is one of the memories of India, as Cawnpore is of England. Cooper's narration reaches its climax in these words:

"There is a well at Cawnpoor; but there is also one at Ujnalla."

I see no reason why he should be denied the immortality he craved so earnestly. Let his name be remembered with Nana Sahib's.

[1] Montgomery Martin, Chapter xxii.

[2] *Letters Written During the Siege of Delhi*, p. 15. H. H. Greathed was acting Civil Commissioner with the besieging army.

IX

So much for the fate of our enemies. What happened to our friends?

"An officer who was attached to Renaud's column told me that the executions of Natives were indiscriminate to the last degree. . . . In two days forty-two men were hanged on the roadside, and a batch of twelve men were executed because their faces were 'turned the wrong way' when they were met on the march. All the villages in his front were burnt when he halted. These 'severities' could not have been justified by the Cawnpore massacre, because they took place before that diabolical act. The officer in question remonstrated with Renaud, on the ground that, if he persisted in this course, he would empty the villages, and render it impossible to supply the army with provisions." [1]

This officer's prophecy was fulfilled. Our forces often had the utmost difficulty in getting supplies, moving through a deserted country. People were chary of proffering food when they knew they would be hanged for their pains. It is amazing that any Indian service was obtained at all.

"The spirit of exasperation which existed against Natives at this time will scarcely be believed in Europe. Servants, a class of men who behaved, on the whole, throughout the Mutiny with astonishing fidelity, were treated even by many of the officers with outrageous

[1] Russell, *Diary*, pp. 221, 222.

harshness. The men beat and ill-used them. In the batteries they would make the bheesties (water-carriers), to whom they showed more kindness than to the rest, sit out of the works to give them water. Many of the unfortunates were killed. The sick syces, grass-cutters, and dooly-bearers, many of whom were wounded in our service, lay for months on the ground, exposed to the sun by day and the cold at night. . . . A general massacre of the inhabitants of Delhi, a large number of whom were known to wish us success, was openly proclaimed. Blood-thirsty boys might be heard recommending that all the Native orderlies, irregulars, and other 'poorbeahs' in our camp should be shot."[1]

In palliation of this state of affairs, Kaye, who quotes the passage, adds:

"I am bound, however, to say that some of my informants, to whom I have referred with especial reference to the alleged inhumanity of our people towards the Natives in camp, are disposed to doubt whether it manifested itself during the siege more strongly than before the mutiny. It is said to have been only the old normal state of things—unaltered, unrepressed."[2]

Majendie, speaking of a comparative lull in the fighting before Lucknow, tells us:

"Still, there was an amount of excitement in it, which kept one up, and which we eked out with a

[1] *The Chaplain's Narrative of the Siege of Delhi*, quoted by Kaye.

[2] Kaye.

certain amusement that we derived from the fright of *khitmudgars* and other native domestics. These poor devils when bringing down their masters' dinners, or employed in similar duties, were unable to keep entirely under cover, but were forced to cross the street, and so run the gauntlet of the enemy's fire, exhibiting during this trying period an amount of terror very entertaining to behold. Their fright we increased sometimes (to our shame be it written) by throwing handfuls of stones close to their feet." [1]

These stones they would take for bullets or showers of grape, and would jump in ecstasy of terror, to the oafish glee of their sheltered masters. If a servant was too fat or too courageous to run, Majendie tells us, someone would often roll a black hooka-bowl against his legs, which would be mistaken for a cannon-ball.

It is mainly of our servants and of villagers who befriended our fugitives that Vincent Smith is thinking when against the misery and cruelty of the Mutiny he sets

"numerous instances of loyalty, kindness, and unselfish devotion which do honour to human nature." [2]

For all Indians did not show themselves "treacherous devils." Many a European life was saved by a great-hearted generosity which risked death for our sakes. That small section of the British community which to-day perpetuates a brutal

[1] *Up Among the Pandies*, p. 211.
[2] *Oxford History of India*, p. 723.

tyranny of attitude and action never wearies of abusing the Indian Christian ; yet many thousands of Indian Christians were put to death by the rebels, for helping us. Nor was it Christians alone who aided the sons and daughters of this most unchristian power.

X

But, after all, the darkest stain on our record is the treatment of the civilian population. Long before the Cawnpore massacre,

"Martial Law had been proclaimed ; those terrible Acts passed by the Legislative Council in May and June were in full operation ; and soldiers and civilians alike were holding Bloody Assize, or slaying Natives without any assize at all, regardless of sex or age. Afterwards, the thirst for blood grew stronger still. It is on the records of our British Parliament, in papers sent home by the Governor-General of India in Council, that 'the aged, women, and children, are sacrificed, as well as those guilty of rebellion.' They were not deliberately hanged, but burnt to death in their villages—perhaps now and then accidentally shot. Englishmen did not hesitate to boast, or to record their boastings in writing, that they had 'spared no one,' and that 'peppering away at niggers' was very pleasant pastime, 'enjoyed amazingly.'"[1]

The reader must be sickened with cruelties. I will give, without comment, merely a few

[1] Kaye, Book V, Chapter ii.

glimpses of our justice operating in different places:

At Benares and Allahabad, before the Cawnpore Massacre.—"On one occasion, some young boys, who, perhaps in mere sport, had flaunted rebel colours and gone about beating tom-toms, were tried and sentenced to death. . . . One of the officers composing the court . . . went with tears in his eyes to the commanding officer, imploring him to remit the sentence passed against these juvenile offenders, but with little effect on the side of mercy. And what was done with some show of formality, either of military or of criminal law, was as nothing, I fear, weighed against what was done without any formality at all. Volunteer hanging parties went out into the districts, and amateur executioners were not wanting to the occasion. One gentleman boasted of the numbers he had finished off quite 'in an artistic manner,' with mango-trees for gibbets and elephants for drops, the victims of this wild justice being strung up as though for pastime, in 'the form of a figure of eight.'"[1]

At Patna: Mr Tayler, Commissioner, and His Method of Getting Evidence.—"I told him, 'I will make a bargain with you; give me three lives, and I will give you yours.' He then told me all the names that I already knew; but could disclose nothing further, at least with any proof in support."[2]

"*At Seharunpore* we found a somewhat vigorous administration, which meant a good deal of hanging.

[1] Kaye, Book V, Chapter ii.

[2] Montgomery Martin, Chapter xx. See also Forrest. Tayler hanged this man.

One junior civilian distinguished himself in that way, and has written a book about it which I have not seen." [1]

At Agra.—" A great many of the villagers in revolt were brought in and hanged, and also some mutinous sepoys who were found lurking in the neighbourhood. When they were being tried, some used to feign madness, and act in the most absurd way, catching flies and jabbering; others would say the most insolent and revolting things to the officers on the court-martial." [2]

At Delhi, after its Capture.—On September 23rd [3] 1857, Mrs Coopland states that the provost-marshal had put to death " between four hundred and five hundred wretches since the siege, and was now thinking of resigning his office. The soldiers, inured to sights of horror, and inveterate against the sepoys, were said to have bribed the executioner to keep them a long time hanging, as they liked to see the criminals dance a 'Pandies' hornpipe,' as they termed the dying struggles of the wretches." Her host, Captain Garstin, had just been to see the Nawab of Jhujjur executed, and reported that he " was a long time dying." [4]

" One day a native jeweller came to offer his wares to Mrs Garstin, who, thinking he charged too much, said, 'I will send you to Metcalfe Sahib'; on which the man bolted in such a hurry that he left his treasures behind, and never again showed his face." [5]

" I saw Sir Theophilus Metcalfe the other day; he

[1] Sir George Campbell, i, 238 (Letter of 12th August 1857).

[2] *A Lady's Escape from Gwalior*, p. 212.

[3] Delhi fell on 14th September 1857.

[4] *A Lady's Escape from Gwalior*, p. 269.

[5] *Ibid.*, p. 273.

is held in great dread here by the natives, and he is every day trying and hanging all he can catch."[1]

"These judges were in no mood to show mercy. Almost all who were tried were condemned; and almost all who were condemned were sentenced to death. A four-square gallows was erected in a conspicuous place in the city; and five or six culprits were hanged every day. English officers used to sit by, puffing at their cigars, and look on at the convulsive struggles of the victims."[2]

"The very regrettable severities at Delhi . . . I was then far away and do not know particulars, but my impression is that many of the executions were unjustifiable."[3]

". . . with the exception of a few days, since the capture of Delhi, there have been five or six executions every day. It is quite impossible to hope to re-establish civil government in that country if the ordinary proceeding of law is to be the infliction of death."[4]

Throughout the North-West Provinces and the Punjab.—"The indiscriminate hanging, not only of persons of all shades of guilt, but of those whose guilt was at the least very doubtful, and the general burning and plunder of villages, whereby the innocent as well as the guilty, without regard to age or sex, were indiscriminately punished, and in some cases, sacrificed, had deeply exasperated large communities not otherwise hostile to the Government; that the cessation of agriculture, and consequent famine, were impending; that there were

[1] Letter from Delhi, in *Times*, January 1858 (Montgomery Martin).

[2] Holmes, p. 386.

[3] Campbell, i, 248.

[4] Lord Ellenborough, in Parliament, on 16th February 1858.

sepoys passing through the country, some on leave, others who had gone to their homes after the breaking-up of their regiments, having taken no part in the mutiny, but having done their utmost to prevent it; others who had risked their lives in saving their European officers from the sanguinary fury of their comrades; and that all of these men, in the temper that at that time generally prevailed among the English officers and residents throughout the country, and still unhappily prevails in some quarters, were liable to be involved in one common penalty; and lastly, that the proceedings of the officers of Government had given colour to the rumour . . . that the Government meditated a general bloody persecution of Mohammedans and Hindus."[1]

XI

All this may be called government by gallows. It was supplemented by government by massacre. Mr "Al. Carthill" tells us:

"Massacre, as part of the activities of Government, is by no means in itself abhorrent to the mind of the Oriental, and the Indian was familiar enough with it. There are several forms of the political massacre, and there was nothing about any of them which was repugnant to the Indian."[2]

It was abundantly put into practice in the Mutiny; at Jhansi, Cawnpore, and Delhi with

[1] Governor-General in Council, 24th December 1857, on state of affairs in the previous July.

[2] *The Lost Dominion*, p. 93.

the justification of massacres to avenge, and at Lucknow without this justification.

"At the time of the capture of Lucknow—a season of indiscriminate massacre—such distinction was not made, and the unfortunate who fell into the hands of our troops was made short work of—sepoy or Oude villager, it mattered not—no questions were asked; his skin was black, and did not that suffice? A piece of rope and the branch of a tree, or a rifle bullet through his brain, soon terminated the poor devil's existence."[1]

At Delhi.—"All the city people found within the walls when our troops entered were bayonetted on the spot; and the number was considerable, as you may suppose, when I tell you that in some houses forty and fifty persons were hiding. These were not mutineers, but residents of the city, who trusted to our well-known mild rule for pardon. I am glad to say they were disappointed."[2]

"Harmless citizens were shot, clasping their hands for mercy. Trembling old men were cut down. But, in justice to the soldiers who committed these cruelties, it should be said that they had received great provocation. Many of their comrades, rashly wandering from their posts, had been enticed by lurking fanatics and budmashes into dark alleys, and there foully murdered."[3]

Patriotism strangely unbalances the sanest minds. This last writer has just told us that our

[1] Majendie, pp. 195, 196.
[2] Letter in the *Bombay Telegraph* (Montgomery Martin).
[3] Holmes, p. 370.

entrance into Delhi was immediately followed by looting of the drink-shops. There was no quarter for any Indian; yet, when our troops, raging, as he has described them, with drink and blood-lust, ran into groups of the men they were thirsting to kill and instead were killed by them, they were "foully murdered" by "fanatics"! What does he think these "fanatics" ought to have done? Apparently they should have led the drunken, disorganised looters gently by the hand back to their own formation, and then delivered themselves up to the provost-marshal. Thus is history set forth and criticised by the author of "the best book" on the Mütiny "for most readers"!

"I have given up walking about the back streets of Delhi, as yesterday an officer and myself had taken a party of twenty men out patrolling, and we found fourteen women with their throats cut from ear to ear by their own husbands, and laid out in their shawls. We caught a man there who said he saw them killed, for fear they should fall into our hands; and showed us their husbands, who had done the best thing they could afterwards, and killed themselves." [1]

"No such scene has been witnessed in the city of Shah Jehan since the day that Nadir Shah, seated in the little mosque in Chandnee Chouk, directed and superintended the massacre of its inhabitants." [2]

[1] Letter in the *Times*, 19th November 1857 (Montgomery Martin.).

[2] Bombay correspondent of the *Times*, 16th November 1857 (Montgomery Martin). This statement needs qualification.

The Oxford History of India[1] has an admirably condensed yet adequate account of the skill and reckless valour which carried Delhi, but not a word that hints at anything beyond the ordinary procedure of civilised troops after taking a city. It is of special interest, therefore, to see what it has to say of Nadir Shah's sack of Delhi in 1739:

"Nadir Shah took terrible vengeance.[2] Seated in the Golden Mosque of Roshanu-ddaula, situated in the main street of the city, he commanded and watched for nine hours the indiscriminate massacre of the people in uncounted thousands. At last he yielded to the prayers of Muhammad Shah and stayed the carnage, which ceased instantly."[3]

We have read contemporary statements which took us back over a century; but there are some which seem to take us forward fifty-seven years, to the frantic misery which accompanied the German invasion of Belgium:

"The people of Delhi had expiated, many times over, the crimes of the mutineers. Tens of thousands of men, and women, and children, were wandering, for no crime, homeless over the country. What they had left behind

Those in arms against us had already fled, except the wounded; and our troops spared the lives of women, massacring the male population only.

[1] P. 716.

[2] For a massacre, as our troops did. "A rising of the inhabitants, in the course of which several hundred of the invaders were killed" (*Oxford History*).

[3] P. 459.

was lost to them for ever; for the soldiers, going from house to house and from street to street, ferreted out every article of value, and smashed to pieces whatever they could not carry away." [1]

"Great numbers of women have thrown themselves on our mercy, and have been safely passed on. One meets mournful processions of these unfortunates, many of them quite unaccustomed to walk, with children and sometimes old men." [2]

"The whole population are being driven out, and they have little chance of seeing their property again. Some old women are found here and there, and are quite kindly treated by the men, and helped out of the place. No instance has yet occurred of any woman being intentionally killed." [3]

I am not prepared to discuss the assurance given me by some of my missionary friends that all this anguish has faded away in two generations from the memory of Delhi, the capital of Indian imagination no less than of Indian story. The new capital of our own empire is rising on foundations of an unforgotten wretchedness. As in places consecrated by great suffering there seems to linger some ghost whose living body bore a part in it, so in the mental atmosphere of Delhi there is to this day something which impalpably but in the end most irresistibly impresses itself on the minds of sensitive English men and women who

[1] Holmes, p. 386.
[2] Greathed, p. 285 (Letter dated 18th September 1857).
[3] *Ibid.*, p. 280 (Letter dated 16th September).

have learned to know its people. Their thoughts are otherwise than those of English men and women who live elsewhere in India—as if for them a veil had been lifted from the unseen. I have felt against them all a patriotic Englishman's exasperation with the fellow-countryman who goes—or seems to go—" native" ; but I now see that they knew more than I did.

XII

But what about Cawnpore, " a memory of fruitless valour and unutterable woe" ? Did not that dreadful scene justify the vengeance of even this war ? I will try to let the reader judge for himself.

" The evidence proves that the sepoy guard placed over the prisoners refused to murder them. The foul crime was perpetrated by five ruffians of the Nana's guard at the instigation of a courtesan. It is as ungenerous as it is untrue to charge upon a nation that cruel deed." [1]

" Women and children would have had a very different prospect of safety and good treatment at the hands of the rebels, had they been viewed as hostages, or any offer of amnesty held out in connexion with them: but in too many of the scattered stations the first phase was blind security; the second, unreasoning panic; the third, martial law, or, in other words, indiscriminate slaughter." [2]

[1] Sir George Forrest, *The Indian Mutiny*, Introduction, xi.
[2] Montgomery Martin, Chapter xvi.

"An Englishman is almost suffocated with indignation when he reads that Mrs Chambers or Miss Jennings was hacked to death by a dusky ruffian; but in Native histories, or, history being wanting, in Native legends and traditions, it may be recorded against our people, that mothers and wives and children, with less familiar names, fell miserable victims to the first swoop of English vengeance;[1] and these stories may have as deep a pathos as any that rend our own hearts. It may be, too, that the plea of provocation, which invests the most sanguinary acts of the white man in this deadly struggle with the attributes of righteous retribution, is not wholly to be rejected when urged in extenuation of the worst deeds of those who have never known Christian teaching."[2]

"It is difficult to say anything in extenuation of the Cawnpore massacre and the terrible scene at the well, and yet we must remember two things: first, that it was done, not in cold blood, but in the moment of rage and despair when Havelock had beaten the rebels and was coming in; and second, that we had done much to provoke such things by the severities of which our people were guilty as they advanced. At a later time a careful investigation was made into the circumstances of the massacre, and we failed to discover that there was any premeditation or direction in the matter. . . . Even discounting a good deal of Kaye's general statements of wholesale atrocities on our part, enough

[1] Kaye is referring to the women and children burnt to death in the villages fired by Neill's column as it advanced on Cawnpore. I have spared the reader an account of these burnings, though eye-witnesses' records are available.

[2] Kaye, Book V, Chapter ii.

remains to make it difficult for us to talk as if the natives only were guilty of deeds of blood. I do not know precisely what happened at Benares, but I suppose the particular things specifically related by Kaye did happen, besides the bloodshed attending Neill's irruption, and I know that at Allahabad there were far too wholesale executions. Again, apart from Neill's doings, and certainly when a Major was sent on by Neill towards Cawnpore, there is no doubt that people were put to death in the most reckless manner. And afterwards Neill did things almost more than the massacre, putting to death with deliberate torture, in a way that has never been proved against the natives." [1]

Sir George Campbell also examines at length the stories current during the Mutiny and, more than anything else, responsible for the ferocity of our actions, of English women being violated as well as murdered. He rejects the stories, in which judgment he is followed by all the reputable authorities.[2]

An Indian who served the Empire long and ably has summarised the Mutiny with a generosity that we look for in vain in the accounts that the victors have given to the world : [3]

"The heroism of the small band of Englishmen who stood at Lucknow against surging masses of insurgents,

[1] Campbell, i, 280.

[2] There is one doubtful case (not mentioned by Campbell), that of Miss Wheeler at Cawnpore. There seems to be some reason for believing that she was not murdered.

[3] Romesh Dutt, *India in the Victorian Age*, p. 224.

and the tragic death of that truest and best of English soldiers, Henry Lawrence, 'who tried to do his duty'; the unflinching courage with which a handful of warriors held their ground through weary months on the historic ridge of Delhi, until the master-hand of John Lawrence denuded the Punjab to deal that memorable blow which decided the fate of the Empire; the rapid and successful march through Central India, and the prolonged and arduous operations in Rohilkhand and Oudh; all these are portions of English history and have been woven into English literature. The Poet-Laureate of the Victorian Age has sung of Lucknow in lines which will never be forgotten; and popular writers of the present day tell the heroic story of John Nicholson and the capture of Delhi.

"Still less is it within the scope of this book to dwell on the darker incidents of the Mutiny; and Englishmen as well as Indians sincerely wish that those incidents could be expunged altogether from history, at least as recorded in school books meant for boys. Wars there have been in India since the days of Clive and Wellington; but never has there been a war stained, on the one side as on the other, by such wanton cruelty and crime as in 1857. . . . The mutineers, rising as they believed in defence of their caste and religion, disgraced and blackened their cause by the inhuman, brutal, and barbarous massacre of defenceless women and children. On the other hand, British troops burnt down villages along their route of many hundreds of miles, turning the country into a 'desert'; British conquerors massacred the inhabitants of Delhi after the mutineers had escaped; and British Special Commissioners executed thousands of citizens in Northern India, guiltless of the Mutiny."

XIII

Sir George W. Forrest's *History of the Indian Mutiny*,[1] which has claims to have superseded Kaye and Malleson's much earlier account as the standard history of the whole episode, manages through three enormous volumes (over fifteen hundred pages) to avoid any reference, however slight and slanting,[2] to excesses or "severities" committed by us. It concludes with an unctuous paragraph on the last three executions, and closes grandly:

> "Justice was done, mercy shown to all who were not guilty of deliberate murder, the land cleansed of blood."[3]

One might throw the lists open to the literature of the whole world, and still not find a more superb example of smug effrontery.

[1] Vols. i and ii, 1904; iii, 1912.

[2] Unless we can accept as such his admission that Lucknow was looted when captured, his statement that on one occasion the *dead* bodies of some sepoys were hung on trees, and his citing with mild disapproval Tayler's offering a man his life in exchange for three lives.

[3] Vol. iii, p. 623.

CHAPTER III

SHADOWS OF THE MUTINY

I

ALL this preceding chapter will by some be considered just a raking up of particularly foul mud that should be allowed to settle. But the raking up is necessary. The raking up of the mud of atrocities committed by Indians has never ceased, as any English account of the Mutiny will show, while the Indian case is not known to our people. I have by no means dredged the Mutiny records for exceptional things that stand to our discredit. I doubt if anything I have brought forward can be called exceptional, except the two cases of tortures inflicted by Sikhs on prisoners, and (possibly) Cooper's action.[1] Our " severities " are patent upon the surface of almost any Mutiny document. They are patent in two books published in 1923—Lord Roberts's *Letters*, and Miss E. Œ. Somerville's *Wheel-Tracks* ; the latter book is eked out with a lot of letters, bloodthirsty in

[1] I have omitted the most shocking cruelty related in his book.

the extreme, by Miss Somerville's[1] uncle. Incidentally, neither book could have been published or praised if in this country there were any regard or chivalrous pity for Indians, or if they were considered fellow-citizens; and both are flagrant examples of book-making, these Mutiny letters being without any literary or other sort of value.[2]

No, the matter could have been set out in a still more unfavourable light. I have left on one side Neill's deeds, which were "almost more than the massacre" of Cawnpore, and Hodson's most notorious atrocity;[3] eyewitnesses' descriptions of villages falling in flames round women and old men have been mercifully omitted. I have not employed Indian testimony. Further, I have hardly drawn a sentence from that sink of ferocity, the Anglo-Indian press, or the scarcely less ferocious press of our own islands. What they said and wrote perished with our fathers, and

[1] One can only suppose that this charming writer—to whom, like the rest of my generation, I am indebted for many delightful hours—did not know the facts; in this respect she was in the same position as the rest of us.

[2] Except in so far as it may be held that even the hastiest scrawls of a great man—Roberts's letters as a very excited and unthinking subaltern—have biographical value.

[3] But I have never understood why this alone, out of the whole Mutiny story, is selected for blame. Is it because the victims were princes? Or because Hodson was unpopular? There is more to be said—even though not much, perhaps—in Hodson's defence than can be said in the case of a thousand actions which are never mentioned.

this age had best forget it; but the deeds, unfortunately, cannot be passed over in silence, for their memory has been burnt into a people's mind.

II

The Mutiny, as I have said, means little to South India. Nor does it as yet mean a great deal to Bengal, though every year it is meaning more. Indeed, in some cases Bengalis in the North-West Provinces perished with us, being killed as our supposed assistants. But from Bihar to the Border the Mutiny lives; it lives in the memory of Europeans and of Indians alike. It overshadows the thought and the relations of both races. A friend who visited the Mutiny country after many years of residence in the South, told me with what a vivid shock this throbbing, tense existence to-day of the agonies of that time was brought home to him. Those memories have never slept, and now they are raising their heads as never before.

Because of the Mutiny a great fear broods over the European community in India, and from time to time, often on very slight provocation, leads to an outcry from "energetic people" for immediate martial law. The Mutiny—that nightmare of innumerable savage hands suddenly upraised to kill helpless women and children—has been responsible for the waves of hysteria which from time to time have swept the European community and for a while made it a pathological case for pity and sympathy. It has done worse than this, however. We are constantly told to-day that the horrible stories of violent crime shown on the cinema create a morbid, dreaming state of mind which loses its hold on normal moral values and leads to repetition of the crimes. And there can be no doubt that the dramatic and heightened fashion in which the Mutiny has been pictured to us has been responsible for deeds that would have been impossible to Englishmen in their right frame of mind. I propose, very briefly, to set out three episodes which (I consider) exemplify this.

III

On the 14th of January 1872 a band of about a hundred Sikh fanatics attacked a Punjab town called Maler Kotla. There was

"a bloody and obstinate fight, with heavy loss on both sides. The survivors, sixty-six in number, including twenty-two who were wounded, fled into the Patiala State. There they surrendered on the 15th of January, and were lodged for the night in the Fort of Sherpore. With their surrender the Kuka rising came to an end.

"On the 16th of January Mr Cowan, who was then Deputy Commissioner of the adjoining British Division of Loodhiana, ordered the prisoners to be sent in to Kotla, where he himself arrived during the day. That evening he wrote to his official superior, the Commissioner, a letter reporting that tranquillity had been completely restored, and adding: 'The entire gang has thus been nearly destroyed. I purpose blowing away from guns or hanging the prisoners to-morrow morning at daybreak.' About noon of the following day (the 17th) he received a note from Mr Forsyth, the Commissioner, desiring him to keep the prisoners at Sherpore till a guard could be sent from Loodhiana. This note, he says, he put in his pocket 'and thought no more about it.' It was not until 4 p.m. on the afternoon of the 17th that the captured Kukas were marched into Kotla, and then and there, without delay or the semblance of a trial, Mr Cowan caused forty-nine of them to be blown away from guns. Close on 7 p.m., when the last batch of six men had been lashed to the guns, there came an official order from Mr Forsyth to send the prisoners to him for trial. In his explanation to Government, Mr Cowan wrote of that order: 'After reading Mr Forsyth's letter, I handed it to Colonel Perkins with the remark that it would be impossible to stay the execution of the men already tied to the guns; that such a proceeding would have the worst effect on the people around us; and so the last six rebels were blown away as had been the forty-three others before them.' One man, who would have made the fiftieth, broke from the guard, rushed at Mr Cowan and caught him by the beard, but was promptly cut down by the sabres of the native officers who were in attendance.

"Such was Mr Cowan's share in this transaction. The Commissioner, Mr Forsyth, had repeatedly enjoined on him to proceed with legal formalities, and on the 17th he telegraphed to the Government: 'I am on the spot, and can dispose of the cases according to form and without delay. Exceptional action not necessary and would increase excitement better allayed.' On the 18th, however, having been informed by Mr Cowan of the ghastly tragedy which had been enacted, he wrote to him in the following terms: 'My dear Cowan, I fully approve and confirm all you have done. You have acted admirably. I am coming out.' He did come out, and sanctioned within the terms of the law the execution of the sixteen remaining prisoners. They were hanged.

"The Government of India recorded an elaborate Resolution on these proceedings. . . . 'His Excellency in Council is under the painful necessity of affirming that the course followed by Mr Cowan was illegal, that it was not palliated by any public necessity, and that it was characterised by incidents which give it a complexion of barbarity.' And so his Excellency was compelled 'with deep regret' to direct that 'Mr Cowan be removed from the Service.' As for Mr Forsyth, he was severely censured and transferred to another province in a corresponding office with the same emoluments.[1] He subsequently became Sir Douglas Forsyth, having been decorated for service beyond the frontier at Yarkand.

"The circumstances of this case and of the orders

[1] "Forsyth appealed against this decision"—*i.e.* his removal from his appointment—"to Lord Northbrook, who had recently come out as Viceroy, and, though no reversal of the verdict was possible, he was compensated by being appointed in 1873 envoy on a mission to Kashgar," *Dictionary of National Biography*, article on Sir Douglas Forsyth. It is perhaps not irrelevant to remember that during the Mutiny Forsyth had been employed as special commissioner to punish the rebels.

passed divided public opinion in India into two camps, in much the same way as Governor Eyre's case had shortly before convulsed public opinion in England. The sympathy of officials generally and of the Anglo-Indian Press was with Messrs Cowan and Forsyth. The Indian Press at this time exercised but a feeble influence, but it raised its voice, such as it was, in horror of what had occurred. For my part, I can recall nothing during my service in India more revolting and shocking than these executions, and there were many who thought, as I did and still think, that the final orders of the Government of India were lamentably inadequate." [1]

There is little to add to Sir Henry Cotton's comments; but, since his judgment may be suspect, I quote Sir Douglas Forsyth:

"As Commissioner and superintendent of the native States, I had the power of life and death which he had not. I wrote to him from Loodiana, ordering him to try the rebels but not to put any sentence into execution until I joined him. But Cowan took the law into his own hands, and put my letter into his pocket, refusing to act on it, and had the men put to death. . . .

"I therefore decided to take upon myself the responsibility of Cowan's act. I wrote a letter approving of what he had done under the circumstances. . . .

"I did my utmost to help him when he was turned out of the service by procuring a very good appointment for him in India." [2]

[1] Cotton, *Indian and Home Memories*. I have used his summary, since I could not improve on its terseness.

[2] *Autobiography and Reminiscences of Sir Douglas Forsyth*, pp. 36, 37, 42.

The vociferous support by the Anglo-Indian press of what it is usual to call "stern justice" and the Government's unwillingness to suggest to Indian opinion that its servants could do wrong are regular features of such cases as this Maler Kotla one. It is an advance upon the Mutiny, fourteen years before, that blowing from guns is at last admitted to be barbarous. But this wholesale execution, without the pretence of a trial, is obviously due to a mind obsessed by those awful "punishment-parades" which were the most dramatic and striking thing in the Punjab tradition of "swift, stern retribution," and which had been praised so often and so enthusiastically. If we are right in thinking that the Napoleonic legend was partly responsible for "Napoleon the Little's" drifting into the Franco-Prussian War, we have far more reason to see the Punjab legend in the actions of this "Little Nicholson."

IV

I do not propose to take the reader through the tangled story of the Second Afghan War of 1879. There was a lull in the war and a treaty, after which Sir Louis Cavagnari was posted at Kabul as our envoy. As Lord Lawrence had foreseen, he and his escort were murdered and the Residency was destroyed. General Roberts acted with the skilful daring that made him famous, and captured Kabul in October. Then came "measures of retribution."[1] There were murders and an insult to our flag to avenge.

"Martial law was established, men were hanged in batches, the Ameer, Yakub Khan, was deported to India, the country was ravaged for supplies, and village-burning was the order of the day."[2]

"I will not find them guilty unless I am convinced of their guilt. The Foreign Office said the punishment should be *short*, *sharp*, and *repressive*. It cannot be *short*, unless we catch men whose guilt is patent. With all others we must enquire thoroughly. I do not believe it ever does good to kill men indiscriminately, and *I will not lend myself to it*."[3]

"October 22nd. Saved five men's lives to-day—that is to say, if I had not inquired into their cases, they would have been hanged. . . . One of the accused was Abu Bakar, a merchant, against whom there was a regular got-up case, the principal witness being his deadly enemy."[4]

"It is to the credit of Sir Donald Stewart that he never tolerated such savage reprisals."[5]

"Nothing can be quieter than the city, which has always been so notorious for bloodshed and turbulence. The shadow of the scaffold is over it, and not one among

[1] *Oxford History of India*, p. 753.

[2] Cotton, *Indian and Home Memories*, p. 172.

[3] *Sir Charles MacGregor* (Roberts's Chief of Staff), *Life and Opinions of*, ii, 136; entry in diary. MacGregor's own italics.

[4] MacGregor, ii, 140, 141.

[5] Cotton, p. 172. Stewart commanded the southern army and in May 1880 superseded Roberts in Kabul.

the ruffians who throng its narrow streets, and hide in its filthy purlieus, but feels its influence. They have hitherto traded upon our known weakness—the worship of the quality of mercy—and it is only now that they understand the new principle of retribution we have introduced into our policy. Like Pollock, General Roberts might have destroyed their bazaar and left Cabul to its fate; but whether we withdraw again or not, there will be the tale of lives taken by our hangmen still to be counted over in the city and the villages; and who knows yet what powerful names may not top the list?"[1]

"What happened? The exasperated tribesmen rose in their thousands; disasters followed in quick succession, redeemed by incidents of splendid courage and devotion; and Lord Roberts found himself besieged under most perilous conditions at Sherpore in the vicinity of Cabul."[2]

"He superintended the compilation of the *History of the Second Afghan War* (6 volumes), which was, however, suppressed by the Indian Government."[3]

The journalist, who (as so often happens) was so much fiercer than many most distinguished soldiers, foretold that the usual noise of protest would be raised by ignorant mugwumps in England, and in a footnote to his foreboding tells us this proved only too true. The only other

[1] *The Afghan War*, 1879–80, p. 139, by Howard Hensman, Special Correspondent of the *Pioneer* (Allahabad) and the *Daily News* (London).

[2] Cotton, p. 172.

[3] *Dictionary of National Biography*, article on Sir Charles MacGregor.

comment that occurs to me is that Afghanistan has been a sullen, treacherous enemy ever since.

The third example of the working of the Mutiny-trained or Mutiny-obsessed mind is Jallianwallabagh, the tragedy of April 1919, under which Indian minds are smarting to-day.

It is necessary to emphasise how terribly difficult General Dyer's position was. At Amritsar —a centre of Sikh fanaticism and patriotism, apart from its unholy connection with Mr Cooper's activities sixty years before—the unrest had got out of hand. The mob had committed atrocious murders, and had tried to commit more. They had tried to set fire to a boarding-school of Christian girls, and it was not their fault that those helpless children had not been burnt to death. Nor was the Jallianwallabagh gathering by any means a peaceful meeting for discussion; nor was it unarmed, except in the sense that there were no firearms. Many of the mob carried *lathis*, the clubs that are the traditional weapon of Indian peasants, with which they had now been murdering people. General Dyer arrived with a small escort, and poured lead into the densely packed sunken garden, inflicting in less than ten minutes casualties roughly equivalent to those the British incurred in the two days of desperate fighting at Spion Kop, the bloodiest battle of the South African War. It may be argued that his action was not governed by strict military necessity, for he fired away all his ammunition, thus jeopardising the grave trusts that were in his hands. His purpose, as stated by himself—and it is generally recognised that he was his own worst enemy, his evidence being given in such a way as to raise one's respect for his courage and honesty but to make his defence a difficult brief to undertake—was to teach the mob a lesson and to strike terror wherever the news penetrated. Other incidents of the episode, such as the absolute neglect of the wounded and the way in which the strict curfew law made it dangerous to bring succour to the tiny place which was left littered with maimed and dead, need not concern us here.

What is immediately relevant is for us to note that at Jallianwalla and during the outcry which our people made afterwards we see the workings of imperfectly informed minds obsessed with thought of Cawnpore and of merciless, unreasoning "devils" butchering our women. Action was taken to stamp out the danger by the methods which were understood to have been efficacious before; and so in a very few minutes fifteen hundred people—Indians claim more, but the official figures, wrung out by public intensity of demand at long last, admit so many—were lying in a garden. Then, when the official mind, which was horrified at the clumsy work of its military colleague but felt obliged to support it, failed to prevent the news from " seeping " through India, percolating rapidly from bazaar to bazaar, till three hundred millions were throbbing and shuddering with a unison they had never known before—no, not once in India's millenniums of history—the European community shook to a tempest of hysterical excitement. What used to be called the " Anglo-Indian "[1] press was filled, especially after the Hunter Committee brought out its very moderate findings, with a shrieking mass of anonymous correspondence—nearly all correspondence in Indian papers is anonymous—from " Britisher," " Old Soldier," " One Who Did His Bit," " One Whose Son Served the Empire." No wonder the Greeks, those careful observers, noted that ghosts have shrill voices. And thirty thousand pounds were collected for General Dyer, largely in India. There must be many a European who was in India then who feels that his community rather made fools of themselves, to put the matter at its lowest.

VI

And we always shall make fools of ourselves, under any sort of provocation, unless we are edu-

[1] " Anglo-Indian " is now the official title of the " domiciled European " community in India.

cated better. It is this that takes away our right to condemn General Dyer's action, for we were all responsible for it. He was our representative, braver than we but certainly not more stupid, and it was our inherited thought concerning the Mutiny and Indians and India that drove him on. The ghosts of Cooper and Cowan presided over Jallianwalla.

I wonder if the reader has yet come to see that there is nothing in our history books more emphatically calling for revision than their accounts of the Mutiny. For, if nothing else has convinced him, let him but consider this ; how confused and contradictory they are. It is only the excitement engendered in the brain by thought of Cawnpore and Meerut that makes it possible for readers, who ordinarily are critical and wide-awake enough, to miss the way in which gaps are slurred over and inconvenient questions begged or burked. Yet, when a period of quiescence under incantation has passed, the mind should sit in judgment on its dream, unless the nerves of waking thought and action are to become diseased. The Mutiny is not yet seventy years old, and the mass of literature contemporary with it is enormous ; yet the episode is less clearly set forth than many that are much further away in time from our day.

Its heroes, too, are monotonous. I remember how the name of John Nicholson fascinated my own boyhood; and I bought the *Life* of him by Trotter which so many possess. But there was no living man in that book; only a conventional, stained-glass saint limned by a very poor artist. There can be few duller books in any language; and, whatever else he was, the real John Nicholson was alive and he was very far from dull. He stirred passionate affection—no, not that, perhaps; but devotion, certainly—and also passionate resentment. He died in the tempestuous sunset of the Mogul day, that day which had been so lurid and glorious; and a mighty city crashed about him as he fell, wrenching its pillars apart. There was a thunderclap prostrating all who heard; and when they looked again, Romulus was gone. What is the good of saying of John Nicholson that "he was a knight belonging to the time of King Arthur rather than to the nineteenth century?"[1] Sir George Campbell, in his testy, querulous fashion, gives us a glimpse of a Nicholson very unlike the pictures—I cannot call them persons—Sir George Forrest thinks he resembled:

"I scarcely knew him personally, but always understood that he was not only vigorous, but even violent in some of his actions and a great deal of his language. And now that we see the things that are told of him by those who most praise him, one cannot but feel that he was a very violent man . . . while Bosworth Smith,

[1] Forrest, i, 117.

in his *Life of Lord Lawrence*, glorifies Nicholson to an excessive degree, some of the facts he relates tell the other way, and it is at any rate clear that he was very insubordinate, and behaved very badly to Lawrence himself." [1]

"Nicholson and some of the more violent men went about calling him [2] an old woman." [3]

"It is perhaps a pity to spoil the stories about the natives worshipping him, which are about as authentic as Highland Jessie, whose best friends now show her, if she ever existed, to have been a Glasgow slavey, and to have derived the divine afflatus from the street music of her native Gallowgate." [4]

Campbell's contempt for the "Nikkul Seyn" stories is not justified; there is good enough evidence for them. He was irritated by the apotheosis of Nicholson, and would have said hard things about "the knight of the time of King Arthur" stuff. But his very prejudice proves that there was an intensely alive personality that provoked it; he had clearly been annoyed by Nicholson's manner when they met, and it must be remembered that during the Mutiny, and for many years after, he was in close touch with many, including Lawrence, who knew Nicholson well. The reader knows that men talk together in a very different fashion, after tennis or

[1] Campbell, i, 248, 249.

[2] Lawrence, who is unanimously admitted to have saved the whole situation.

[3] Campbell, i, 235.

[4] *Ibid.*, p. 249.

dinner—and how often must Nicholson have been discussed, by men who had known him or were interested in the events which made him famous!—from the way they express themselves in official papers. At any rate, if Mr Lytton Strachey ever contemplates a second group of "Eminent Victorians," I can point out to him an interesting subject.

In the same way there are popular books from perusal of which one rises with the impression that Neill[1] and Havelock and Hodson, and others

[1] For Neill, the reader must look up his record for himself, and then choose between the glorification of such writers as the Rev. W. H. Fitchett and Mr Holmes, and the opinion of Campbell. Neill's doings outside Benares move Holmes to one of his brilliant *non-sequiturs*: "In fact, Neill had inspired the populace with such terror that a rumour arose that the English were going to bombard the city; and many of the citizens fled with their families into the country. At no epoch of history has individual character achieved more extraordinary results than in the course of the Indian Mutiny" (p. 219). Sir George Campbell says: "Neill is one of those people who have been elevated into a hero on the strength of a feminine sort of violence, and whose death much disarmed criticism at the time, but now that he has passed into old history, I may say that, so far as I could learn from the most impartial sources, there was not much more in him . . . I can never forgive Neill for his very bloody work, and especially for his share in the mismanagement which caused the loss of the regiment of Loodiana. At Allahabad, by violence and mistrustful usage, he all but turned against us the Ferozepore regiment (only second to the men of Loodiana in my affection) which afterwards did such splendid service" (i, 281, 282).

who are great Mutiny names, divided their time between singing hymns and receiving devout and worshipping affection from their soldiers. From a very fleeting study of contemporary documents one can gather that they had other activities.

VII

Some day we shall have a reading public who will see that the Mutiny, interpreted in terms of the old story of the battle between the Angels of Light and the Angels of Darkness, is as dull as Milton's angelic battles. For where Milton failed, our Fitchetts have certainly not succeeded. If "Jack Pandy" was simply a cowardly traitor, where was the merit in storming his entrenchments? Every form of exercise is in its degree exciting, even rabbit-shooting; but it by no means follows that books about rabbit-shooting are exciting. We all know the traditional way of writing about the Mutiny:

"With brand upraised and white plume flashing far,
What haughty chieftain holds the front of war? [1]
Well knows the foe that warrior in the fight,
Stern as the storm and terrible as night;
Not his to dread the battle's blood-red waves,
Nor the wild rush of Heaven-detested slaves. . . ." [2]

[1] The answer, of course, is John Nicholson.

[2] *Delhi and Other Poems*, by Charles Arthur Kelly, M.A., Bengal Civil Service.

How often, in the early days of the War, our newspapers told us that German soldiers had to be beaten into battle by their officers! But this belief was not held at the front. Nor did our newspaper men produce very interesting books on the War.

There are the faint beginnings of chivalry here and there in the suppressed admiration with which some of our historians speak of the Rani of Jhansi. She was the "best and bravest" of the rebel leaders, her conqueror, Sir Hugh Rose, said bluntly, saying more than was true. It is not easy for an Englishman to think, without the beginnings of pity, of a young and very lovely woman who rode out against us and died fighting, her sister,[1] as resolute and beautiful as herself, beside her in life and in death. To Indians she is their Joan of Arc. And one day we shall ask ourselves if we do not wish to be informed more truthfully of that intensity of hatred which led even women—even Indian women—to take arms against us; the Rani and her sister were by no means the only women who fought in the Mutiny. At Jhansi took place

> "a perfidious massacre of the Europeans, men, women, and children, comparable in wickedness with the slaughter at Cawnpore, but on a smaller scale."[2]

[1] Or, perhaps, her co-wife. We do not know the relationship of these two young women to each other.

[2] *Oxford History*, p. 721.

The Rani, who took over the reins of state three days later, has never been cleared of suspicion of complicity in the massacre. I think it reasonable to assume, from her subsequent bitterness of opposition to the race she hated, that the massacre had her entire approval; and her father was one of the very many whom we sent to the gallows after Jhansi fell. Yet for a long time now Mutiny historians have made allowances for the Rani's hatred and have spoken of her valour with admiration. If the process begins with the Rani, it cannot end with her. Montgomery Martin,[1] writing towards the end of the Mutiny, points out how even the Anglo-Indian press was beginning to admire another rebel leader, Prince Firoz Shah. He was believed to have done his best to prevent the Delhi massacre[2] of our people, and he showed himself in the field as valiant and steadfast as any hero on our side, though he knew he was fighting for a hopeless cause and that if captured he could only expect the gibbet or the cannon's mouth. It was a relief to many, even of his foes, that we never captured this brave and skilful man. His horsemanship and his hair-breadth escapes became a legend. He is believed

[1] Chapter xxvi.

[2] This seems a mistake. Apparently he was on pilgrimage at Mecca, landing in India after the Mutiny had broken out, and hurrying to the front of what he considered a war for independence. The massacre was then over.

to have lingered in India till 1864, a fugitive in its forests, and he was last heard of in 1866, as a beggar in Arabia.[1] Here, at least, the "cowardly Pandy" talk is far astray:

> "Crazed, if you will; demented, not to yield[2]
> Ere all be lost! And yet it seems to me
> He fought as noblest Englishmen did use
> To fight, for freedom; and no Briton he,
> Who to such valour in a desperate field
> A knightly salutation can refuse."[3]

VIII

And some day—a century hence, perhaps—Indian traditions and accounts of the Mutiny will be taken into the reckoning. It will be treated as history, not prejudice or propaganda. It will become a terrible but most enthralling story. But we shall no longer feel free to dismiss even the sack of Cawnpore with

"The justly infuriated troops took terrible vengeance";[4]

or,

"On the 16th of July, General Havelock defeated Nana Sahib at Cawnpore; the city was occupied by the

[1] A considerable group of exiles gathered in Arabia, refugees from the Mutiny.

[2] Yet, as I have pointed out, this resource was denied him.

[3] Sir William Watson, *The Enemy*. I have changed *they* to *he*.

[4] *Oxford History*, p. 719.

English, and a sanguinary, but well-merited, retribution exacted."[1]

Nor will the well-known tepid quality of its writer's thinking induce readers to pass this *résumé* of the whole bitterly felt episode:

"Summary vengeance was inflicted on the sepoy rebels, which gave rise to some criticism of our troops for inhumanity; but Lord Canning, the Governor-General, was no less severely blamed for his clemency; and the general verdict was in favour of the measures adopted by the military and civilian officers, whose zeal and capacity suppressed the Mutiny."[1]

That kind of writing is not history, and it would not be tolerated on any other theme. Indian reverence for Queen Victoria ensured in advance that her *Letters* would be read eagerly by her Eastern subjects. This fact makes the more culpable the writer's neglect of an editor's elementary duty of making himself more or less conversant with the subject-matter and sources of his generalisations.

IX

I do not forget the provocation which in part excuses our ruthlessness. It is that provocation which saves the story from being one of unrelieved gloom for the Englishman who loves

[1] *Letters of Queen Victoria*, edited by Arthur Christopher Benson, M.A., and Viscount Esher, G.C.V.O., K.C.B., iii, 224.

and believes in his race. The sepoys, in the words, already quoted, of an Indian,[1]

"disgraced and blackened their cause by the inhuman, brutal, and barbarous massacre of defenceless women and children."

That side has received abundant attention. Yet even this record of mutinies and massacres needs more critical treatment than it has yet had if we are to be just. The murders with which the Mutiny began, those of Meerut, were the work of a small body of troops, infuriated by what they considered a vindictive punishment and maddened by fear of loss of caste. The massacre which followed fast on its heels, that of Delhi, was done at the instigation of this body of men, and it stands apart with an atrocity of its own. Then, when almost the whole sepoy army—as whole regions were swept into anarchy—mutinied, often after long hesitation, in twenty-two stations and was drawn into one gulf of condemnation, atrocity and counter-atrocity acted and reacted. The two cruellest massacres of Europeans, those of Jhansi and Cawnpore, occurred long after a policy of indiscriminate vengeance had been put into operation. It is certain that the historian of the future will not acquit Neill of some responsibility for the tragedy he avenged and punished so dreadfully.

[1] Romesh Dutt.

Also, though our historians are so fond of asserting that the Mutiny was not a war of independence, but purely a military sedition, our action in hanging many thousands of citizens after travesties of trial or none at all, and burning villages of friends as well as foes, with any race but Indians would have turned the Mutiny into a general rising of the civil population. As it is, even though the Agra Province "became 'a sea of anarchy,'"[1] the civil population, as a whole, were very far from being carried away by the cruel hatred of either side; and it is to their credit that they saved so many fugitive Europeans and that the "blood-money," offered by both sepoys and Indian Government, was so very rarely earned from either.

"*In the course of ten days English administration in Oudh had vanished like a dream, and not left a wrack behind. The troops mutinied, and the people threw off their allegiance; but there was no revenge and no cruelty. The brave and turbulent population, with a few exceptions treated the fugitives of the ruling race with marked kindness, and the high courtesy and chivalry of the Barons of Oudh was conspicuous in their dealings with their fallen masters, who, in the day of their power, had from the best motives inflicted on many of them a grave wrong.*"[2]

We can recognise, too, that both sides were maddened out of their minds by beliefs that were

[1] *Oxford History.*

[2] Forrest, i, 217.

not true. Many of the rebels believed that we aimed at a general extirpation of all Hindus and Mohammedans, or a subversion of their religions. And our own literature reveals what wild stories of diabolical cruelty, beyond the dreams of previous ages almost, were accepted as fact by our race. And such stories will always have an easy passage to credulity, until men train themselves to wait and think at times of excitement. Passion is the highroad on which propaganda travels. The German public accepted statements about Belgians which stirred their soldiers to ferocity and were partly responsible for the iniquities which all the world knows. Europe believed the wildest slanders about us in the South African War. Whenever a war breaks out, both sides immediately bring charges of violated neutrality and the like, and both sides have no difficulty in getting almost unlimited credence. Even in time of peace the mass of people remain singularly incurious. Our opportunities for sifting evidence are often so slight, our inclinations often slighter.

At the time of Amritsar, too, the feeling of the European community was similarly aroused, and in part justified. More than the murders by the mob, the attack on an English lady—and that lady one who was devoting her life to the service of their own women—and the placards inciting to the dishonouring of English women, raised anger to boiling-point. In this latter respect the rioters—rebels, if you like; I think they certainly were—went beyond anything proved against the Cawnpore murderers. Only the most criminal elements[1] in the mob, of course, were responsible for this; but my impression at the time was, and is now, that even the most sensitive and noble Indians failed to realise the depth of British feeling on this matter, or to see why we consider that dishonour and suffering is so much worse when inflicted on a woman than when inflicted on a man. It may be that an absolute code of ethics would not uphold our feeling; it may be, as we are often told to-day, that our sentiment is a sham and hypocrisy, a false glamour flung about women by an age of barbarism which we call the age of chivalry. But it will not be easy to dispel from the European mind the conviction that this sentiment is the most precious gift to us from the confused and often mistaken thinking of our mediæval forefathers, and that it has done infinitely more to purify and ennoble life than all the *satis*[2] that ever took place. At any rate, the cleavage is there, and it is well to beware of it.

[1] But those were numerous.

[2] *Suttees.*

XI

It is impossible to overestimate the harm done by the hysterical way in which the European community rushed to the defence of the Punjab repressions, and especially Jallianwalla. This excitement was far from universal, however, though Indians must have thought it was. I have heard many Army officers speak about Jallianwalla justly and moderately; and among Government officials, at any rate outside the Punjab, I believe the same judicial, balanced view held. But these by the rules of their services are a silent body, and it was not their voice that Indians heard.

It is often good for Englishmen in the East to live among the people; it is nearly always bad for them to live together. In the Mutiny, scattered and tiny groups of our countrymen acted with a calm heroism that we should impoverish ourselves by forgetting, while Calcutta—which was "as safe as houses," with troops continually pouring through—and (to a much less extent and with more justification). Simla disgraced themselves by hysterical panic and that hysterical cruelty of spirit which springs from terror. As Canning wrote to Queen Victoria,

> "To those whose hearts have been torn by the foul barbarities inflicted upon those dear to them any degree of bitterness against the natives may be excused. No

man will dare to judge them for it. But the cry is raised loudest by those who have been sitting quietly in their homes from the beginning and have suffered little from the convulsions around them unless it be in pocket. It is to be feared that this feeling of exasperation will be a great impediment in the way of restoring tranquillity and good order, even after signal retribution shall have been deliberately measured out to all chief offenders." [1]

Canning proved only too good a prophet when he wrote, in the same letter:

"One of the greatest difficulties which lie ahead—and Lord Canning grieves to say so to your Majesty—will be the violent rancour of a very large proportion of the English community against every native Indian of every class . . . nor does it occur to those who talk and write most upon the matter that for the Sovereign of England to hold and govern India without employing, and, to a great degree, trusting natives, both in civil and military service, is simply impossible. It is no exaggeration to say that a vast number of the European community would hear with pleasure and approval that every Hindoo and Mohammedan had been proscribed, and that none would be admitted to serve the Government except in a menial office. That which they desire is to see a broad line of separation, and of declared distrust drawn between us Englishmen and every subject of your Majesty who is not a Christian, and who has a dark skin; and there are some who entirely refuse to believe in the fidelity or goodwill of

[1] *Letters of Queen Victoria*, iii, 251.

any native towards any European; although many instances of the kindness and generosity of both Hindoos and Mohammedans have come upon record during these troubles."

So, during the excitement arising after the Punjab happenings, it was not the district official, or the missionary, or the planter[1] in a lonely station, men living in daily contact with Indians and really in danger of their lives if a second Mutiny came, who squealed and shrieked, but the people who lived together in hill-stations or large towns, where regular troops and volunteer forces were within easy summons. And a great deal of this was due to the same cause as much of the bitterness felt by Indians—the feeling of powerlessness. The district official or planter is not powerless; he has his experience and his knowledge of himself, of a self which daily emergency has brought well within and under its own instinctive control, and he has his knowledge of the people and many friendships among them. Even if, in some sudden gust of cruel madness, they were to kill him, his ghost, could it speak, would not cry for indiscriminate vengeance, for he knows that a community may be imbrued in blood by the guilt of a very few. But in the hill-stations and the large towns our people live a life cut off from the main life of the great

[1] I am thinking of the best type of planter—an extraordinarily fine type, with an intimate, silent knowledge of the people.

country where they are sojourning, they are ignorant as regards India, and disfranchised as regards the Empire. They have only their petty social imitations of London, their silly "social intelligence," their patter of how Mrs Jones "looked effective in white charmeuse," or how Miss Dorrit and Mr Doolittle won the affinity stakes at the gymkhana; or, if they are outside this circle, they have the doings of this circle to read about. Their booksellers provide for them the books that England finished with a year ago. Their newspapers dole them out such news as the editors choose—during the Punjab excitements it was chiefly extracts from the *Morning Post*, so that the community never realised how deep and wide was the cleavage between them and their countrymen at home. They pass resolutions from time to time—at least, the European Association passes them for them—and these are sent home, where they have as much attention as if they came from Kamschatka. Even General Dyer's thirty thousand pounds was largely the result of a subconscious argument: "This'll be a slap in the face for that fellow Montagu! A Jew Secretary of State for India! We'll show him what we think of his so-called Reforms!" It was all they could do; they have no vote that matters, and no Cabinet ever gives a second's thought to their wishes when a Secretary of State for India is appointed.

The tension existing in India has been bad for our race; and a conception of Indian life based upon the writings of Ethel M. Dell or Maud Diver, or even Kipling, has not helped. We have become so much raw material for "mass-suggestion"; our newspapers first discover—an easy matter—the direction in which our herd-psychology will drive us most readily and swiftly, and then "shoo" and stampede us that way. Indians, known only as beggars in the street or as cringing suppliants for our favour, or seen (with that "inward eye" which can be so many things besides "the bliss of solitude") as the men who did unspeakable things at Cawnpore, are regarded with suspicion and hatred.

It is a bad country for our women, too; and it is becoming worse. For a woman it is tolerable only if her husband's salary is sufficient to afford her the comfort and service that are daily becoming more expensive, or if she has very strong intellectual interests. The right kind of woman, combining with her grace of womanliness a grace of freedom such as Indian culture denies to its own women, wins from Indians, whether her husband is official or planter or missionary, nothing less than worship. But too often women become fretful and full of suspicion. Nothing throughout the Punjab controversy was more passionately resented by Indians, especially by Indian women, than the prominent part our own women took in the defence of Jallianwalla. For every Indian woman knew that this was the kind of thing that had happened:

"'When did you come to know of your husband's having been killed in the square?' 'Soon after the firing I heard in my street that thousands had been killed. I got very anxious, and I thought of going to the square at once. Two female neighbours went with me. I saw the whole place full of dead bodies. I went round and looked for my husband among the dead bodies. I had to pull out my husband's body from under a heap of dead bodies. There were pools of blood all over the place.'

"The witness then described her failure to get help to carry her husband's body home. She continued: 'I turned back and came to the side of my husband's dead body. I remained watching there the whole night. I had to watch the dead body with a stick in hand because there were dogs about. At about 2 a.m. I heard the groans of a wounded Sikh. I went to his help and put his wounded leg in position. There was a wounded boy of twelve years of age who kept crying the whole night. He was entreating me the whole time not to leave the place, as he was very much terrified. There was another man crying for water in a most piteous manner. No water was to be had there, and I felt helpless. Except the cries of the wounded, the only thing that I heard was the barking of dogs and the braying of donkeys. At 6 a.m. Sundar Das came with a cot. We then brought the dead body of my husband home and later took it to the cremation-ground.'"[1]

[1] O'Dwyer V. Nair, *Times Report*, 28th May 1924.

Fortunately, there are a great many Indians who realise that in India, as a community, we show at our worst; and when they are most bitter some saving memory of the greatness and generosity of England's record slips in between their mind's thought and its utterance.

XII

But the community which suffers most from the Mutiny obsession is the Eurasian. That community has received grave wrong at our hands. By a process of the most shameful neglect and active contempt it has been reduced to its weak and dependent condition; and out of weakness spring bitterness and an aching wretchedness of mind. It might have been a bridge between the two races now so estranged; instead, it has become a source of exasperation to both. In old days it rendered very great service to the British Raj; and many honoured names in our Indian history show what vigour of will and intellect Eurasians have possessed. Nor was its gift to the Indian community less, in such personalities as Derozio's. Yet to-day the Eurasian community is regarded by Indians with a hatred which is rarely felt by them for the British; and with the British they carry, in the stigma of "native blood," a disability as cruel and unjust as it is crushing. They feel they must cling to us; and they do it in a weak, helpless, noisy way. Their loyalty—why *should* they give us such loyalty when we have treated them as we have ?—is beyond any loyalty that we get from the free races of our world-wide Commonwealth. As recently as the Great War they gave abundant proof that they can take their place with "the steadfast among spears" as resolutely as any Britisher of us all. If our Empire, which spends so freely on armaments and advertisement, would spend a comparatively small sum on education and facilities for this despised community, we should be strengthened very greatly; and at the same time there would be a great cleansing of the waters of bitterness in India, and a great lifting of mists that darken Indian minds and ours.

XIII

See then what long shadows the Mutiny and, still more, our misrepresentation of the Mutiny have cast through two generations! We would repudiate the suggestion that our Empire is a rule of masters over slaves. Yet we judge as slave-drivers would, and assess the virtues of our fellow-citizens as a hunter assesses those of dogs. The great question is, Is an Indian loyal? Is he "true to his salt?" It does not matter whether that salt has been made unnecessarily bitter, as it was by the enforced usage of the greased cartridges. Whatever happens, whatever causes of grievance some incredible stupidity may have forced upon them, still—are they loyal? As a chaplain of the Indian Ecclesiastical Establishment —that exacting service—asked a friend of mine, who was trying to explain to him that Rabindranath Tagore was a considerable literary man, "But is he *loyal*?" That was the only point of interest. The inquirer was a man with the brains of a rabbit; but still, he accepted it as without question that he somehow exemplified a pattern wisdom and civilisation to which every Asiatic must render unquestioning obedience. If it had been St Paul who was a subject of the British Empire to-day he would have asked the same question. But he would never dream of asking it about a Canadian or Australian. Indians are asking to-day, Have we ever given them any real *citizenship*? Nothing in the Punjab happenings, except perhaps the "crawling" order, hurt more closely than the bombing of towns. They argued: It is conceivable that you might shoot down a mob in Glasgow or Liverpool; but you would never use bombs except on a people against whom you had declared war.

I submit to all English men and women who desire to think and act fairly that it is "not good enough." There are other merits in an Indian fellow-citizen more honourable and altogether more consistent with our own self-respect than the servile deference which we call loyalty. But, of course, if we cannot look upon any Indian except as so much crude oil for the flames of rebellion and mutiny, as the possible participant in another Cawnpore massacre, then there is only one merit that he can show. Is he *loyal*?

XIV

I am not going to say much about the influence of the Mutiny and its memories on the Indian mind. Any reader with imagination can guess. When two nations war, any amount of bloodshed in battle is forgiven and forgotten. But when one side sets itself up as a tribunal, and takes upon itself the wholesale use of the gallows and firing-squad, then it does something that is not forgiven or forgotten while the generations last. There is more bitterness in France over the execution of the *franc-tireurs* than over all the bloodshed of Gravelotte and Mars-la-Tour. The shooting of Captain Fryatt will be remembered with deep, glowing anger when Ypres is only a glorious memory. The Sikhs whose thousands had perished in battle a dozen years before were our friends in the Mutiny; but the blood of the fifty whom Cowan blew to pieces has set a gulf between them and us to-day. Nathan Hale, Major André, Wolfe Tone, Pearse—what memories of hatred these names keep alive! And when military executions have been crushed out of official existence and are unrecognised in the text-books they live from generation to generation, as the Mutiny ones do in the bazaars of Northern India. Is it not possible that here is a fire of smouldering bitterness which owes nothing to "Panditji's" stoking? Had not the men whom we shot and hanged, often after the mockery of a trial or none at all, families and friends; and are not their sons living to-day?

"The head of the family, like his own father, was stern and orthodox to the point of fanaticism. A strain of moroseness, almost of madness, had marked him ever since the day when his father-in-law had been put to death on charges connected with the Mutiny of 1857."[1]

"It is difficult, perhaps, to read the elusive Eastern mind. No one can be quite sure what lies in its mysterious chambers. But that the memory of the Mutiny lives, and lives with a certain bitter flavour in the popular mind, is certain. A missionary told the present writer that in his earlier and less experienced days he instructed his class of catechists to write an essay on the Mutiny. Every youth sent in a sheet of blank paper! It was a silent, unanimous, and unapologetic refusal to perform the task."[2]

[1] *Tilak*, by Winslow (Oxford University Press). This is the Christian poet Tilak, a close kinsman of the famous nationalist.

[2] W. H. Fitchett, *The Tale of the Great Mutiny* (6th impression), pp. 440, 441.

It is maintained by some of the few Englishmen who know the truth of what happened in 1857, that all that is necessary is to wait a few years more, till the memories have died with the minds that store them. But that is not the case. So long as the story is told by our books as it is now, the resentment will spread and grow. It is felt over a wider area to-day than it was twenty years ago. In considering English politics, we have readjusted our ideas from the times of Gladstone and Lord Salisbury; yet we never seem to readjust them with regard to India. Indian disunity and dissension is a favourite theme of our publicists; but India grows daily in consciousness of her unity. The agony endured by Oudh seventy years ago is resented to-day far beyond the borders of Oudh; the name of Delhi lights a spark even in the mind of the Hindu Dravidian south. There are only two ways of assuaging this bitterness: either let us close all schools and colleges, put down with heavy penalties all learning to read or write, and as far as we can, banish all thinking and discussion, every sort of education; or let us face the things that happened, and change our way of writing about them.

The bitterness is often most deeply felt by Indians in England. Vinayak Savarkar, now serving a life-sentence in the Andamans for complicity in the murder of Sir Curzon Wyllie, was a student in London. What made him an irreconcilable there, amid the frank kindliness that so many Indians have testified to receiving in England? The answer lies in what was his absorbed study. Sir Valentine Chirol calls his *War of Indian Independence of 1857*,

"in its way a very remarkable history of the Mutiny, combining considerable research with the grossest perversions of facts, and great literary power with the most savage hatred."[1]

Readers may remember his attempt to escape when being taken out to India for trial; he jumped from the ship and swam ashore at Marseilles, being handed back, after hesitation and discussion, as a man accused of a felony and not a political offence. Without palliating his crime, Englishmen may regret that our Empire can do nothing with a youth who combined such pluck with "great literary power," but send him to penal servitude for life. He entered caves of forbidden history, holding high the torch of his blazing hatred; and he descried all the deeds which we hoped would never be seen. He read our cold, insolently self-righteous accounts of that most wretched and brutal war; and a madness worked in his brain, which ended in a murder which—with some people, at any rate—shadows Indians studying in our midst to-day.

[1] *Indian Unrest*, p. 149.

SHADOWS OF THE MUTINY

XV

Savarkar's *History* of the Mutiny is proscribed. It is best that it should be. But if we wish to have a veil drawn over certain aspects of that war, we must give the Indian case recognition in our own histories. As things stand, we have given Indians a reputation for bloodthirstiness and untrustworthiness which they are very far from deserving.

> "Few Indians are cruel in the sense that we use that term. To see blood and suffering rarely gives pleasure to the Indian, whether a Hindu or a Moslem of Indian ancestry. Exceptions there have been, no doubt, some of the Moslem rulers in particular having been victims of the blood-lust, but it will generally be found that cruelty in India has been the work of alien races, particularly that of the Finno-Ugrian stock—the Turk. Still less it is a pleasure to the Indians to commit atrocities." [1]

Our misrepresentation of Indian history and character is one of the things that have so alienated the educated classes of India that even their moderate elements have refused to help the Reforms. Those measures, because of this sullenness, have failed, when they deserved a better fate.

[1] *The Lost Dominion*, p. 91. The English of the last sentence is remarkable; but this may be due to "Al. Carthill's" compositor.

And Indians misrepresent us, taking revenge in their turn. The most widely read of their monthlies has always seemed to me a study in steady, conscienceless misrepresentation. Indians, taxed with this, will admit it ; but add, " It is the same in all politics. All is fair in love and war." When the English Government objected to the French invasion of the Ruhr, this monthly said it was because they were afraid the French were going to get all the trade of the Ruhr. If we had not protested, it would have been because we were allied with the French in crushing a helpless foe. When the United States High Court decided against Indian rights of citizenship, it was in obedience to the wishes of the British Consul in Washington, whose mission was poisoned by England's rancour against India ! This last misrepresentation was a little too grotesque, and an Indian in America wrote, drawing attention to a similar decision against the Japanese and asking if the British Consul had been responsible for that also. When there is a students' strike, it is always assumed that the authorities have been guilty of the grossest tyrannies. When a mass of students on strike, not satisfied with " non-violent " obstruction which took the form of lying across all the paths leading to the college, rolled themselves against the feet of a missionary principal whose record of unselfish service Indians gladly acknowledge, then (according to Calcutta dailies) he had "kicked and trampled upon them in the most brutal manner." Nor is the worst mischief done in India. Germany and the United States have been particularly fruitful fields for slander. When some of us were trying to get our countrymen to see what injustice Indians had suffered in the Punjab, our task was rendered too hard and disheartening for words by the volunteer assistance that came from America, particularly from an organisation calling itself the "American Home Rule League for India"[1] (or some such name), and a reverend gentleman who (as Mr Churchill said of Mr Joseph Chamberlain, no doubt very wrongly) "stood no nonsense from facts." Our foes in derision quoted his statistics of some thousands of dead—I forget how many—and refused to face the very real and horrible fact that fifteen hundred people had been shot down in a few minutes. This atmosphere of misrepresentation by Indians and their sympathisers has become a stifling air to many a man who wishes India well; and it has robbed Indians of a great deal of the assistance they think they ought to receive from us in their struggle for self-government. We love the cause, and have proved our love; *sed non tali auxilio.* And many an Englishman who is

[1] I wish—and many Indians wish—that American friends of freedom would leave India alone. It is not their business; and they can find useful occupation much nearer to their famous statue of Liberty.

rendering India the most unsparing and genuine service feels that his task is becoming too embittered for continuance.

It comes down to this, that men and women everywhere want their self-respect given back to them. Make them free again, and enable them to look us and everyone in the eyes, and they will behave like free people and cease to lie. There is long overdue a new orientation in the histories of India. We must no longer stress the Black Hole of Calcutta, and ignore the seventy suffocated Moplah prisoners of our railway-vans; we must no longer stress Cawnpore, and ignore Benares and Delhi and Allahabad and Renaud's march on Cawnpore. If there was one phrase more than another in Romesh Dutt's dignified appeal to us which should win our respectful sympathy it was his request that the darker incidents of the Mutiny (or such as we choose shall be told) should be expunged from books, "at least as recorded in school books meant for boys." Why should Indian boys be compelled to read about the fiendish work at the well, when there is not a word said about Neill's fiendish work on the way to the well?

I believe there never was a time when my own people were more willing to redress old wrongs; and there is within them, as Indians know and in their heart of hearts believe, a chivalry which will scorn to inflict upon a weaker people a distorted account of their own actions. It is only necessary for my race to understand what has been done in its name, for them to make short work of the fiction and the "history" that they have been giving their own boys and forcing upon Indian boys reading in the schools we have established.

Lastly, let us publish no more Mutiny letters when we know that similar documents from the Indian side if published would be immediately proscribed as fomenting racial hatred.

CHAPTER IV

CONCLUSION

But I am not content to leave the matter so. There are a few other things that should be said, as briefly as possible. First, in " Al. Carthill's " statement that government by massacre does not stir any deep repugnance in Indians there is some truth, as in a great many of this shrewd if reckless writer's observations. The East India Company was the successor of the Mogul Empire, and it wrought after its ways. Instead of impaling and flaying alive, it put to death in other fashion; under both rules, districts where rebellion had taken place were depopulated and pillaged. That was two hundred years ago and seventy years ago; and in the British connection with India seventy years is the equivalent of five hundred in Europe. Antiquity is relative; and already there is an immeasurable gap between the thinking of our fathers and our thinking. Cowan's massacre in 1872, it is probable, shocked Indians and some Englishmen far more than anything that the latter did in 1857; so far had the time-spirit carried his children in fourteen years. When indignation surges in Indian breasts to-day, it is partly because they are looking at the Mutiny not with their countrymen's mind of seventy years ago, but with their mind of to-day, a mind that has been nourished and trained by our own noblest literature and history. They judge us by our own standards; but the worst doings of the Moguls are relegated frankly to a barbarism which has perished. Yet the rough and ready efficiency of John Company's rule, and its occasional outbreaks of ferocity, are almost equally far away from to-day; they can never be repeated, they are both something alien to our thought and habits.

We can undoubtedly cleanse this poisoned well. There are many Indians, and an increasing number of Englishmen, who wish with all their hearts that the Mutiny might be passed over as quickly and lightly as possible, and the natural kindliness of both races given a free way. "In the interests of India and England it is best that the bitter memories of that cruel rebellion should be forgotten."[1] Only—it must be passed over by *both* sides.[2]

[1] C. T. Metcalfe (son of the Theophilus Metcalfe mentioned already), p. 1, "Introduction," *Two Native Narratives of the Mutiny in Delhi*.

[2] For an example of the way exasperation is kept alive, take the inscription on the notorious statue of Lawrence in Lahore (which has to be guarded from the anger of Indians). "The artist represents John Lawrence as offering to the people the choice between enforced submission and willing obedience:

As Indians become more and more citizens of the whole world, so that to them history is not simply a record of themselves and the English, they will see that even these anguished memories must be seen not isolated but in the context of their age. It is our glorification of the Mutiny that is exceptional, not its brutality. It was an age when war was savage and unchivalrous, when Austrians executed Hungarians and Russians Poles, when Carlists and their foes shot and hanged each other in Spain, when (as in 1871) civil strife in Paris was wholesale butchery and reprisal. They and we are entitled to refuse to accept responsibility for deeds done before we were born, if we are resolute to prove that our thoughts now move in a nobler world. Also, in the Mutiny, as so often in controversy between nations, different ethics were involved. We are far more of a military nation than we sometimes recognise; and to a military nation mutiny is the gravest of crimes, involving the instant forfeiture of the mutineer's right to exist, irrespective of how hardly he may have been used before he mutinied. But the unquestioned ethics of one society are very questionable indeed to another. To a king

'By which will ye be governed—the pen or the sword?' The pen prevailed; but none the less was the sword ever in reserve, though sheathed" (Sir Charles Aitchison, *Lord Lawrence*, pp. 50, 51, "Rulers of India" series). Some of the things done in the name of Britain are incredible.

and to a philosopher rebellion shows very diversely, as heresy does to an inquisitor and to a scientist. Men in perfect sincerity have broken to pieces other men as sincere as themselves, and have done it in the names of right and of God. Our cause is never so right, or our enemies' cause so wrong, as our conscience asserts.

Particularly, I would urge my fellow-Christians to take this matter to heart, and to see to it that among them there is a change of attitude towards India. I will tell them what is never told them in missionary conferences or from missionary platforms, that the great obstacle to the outward acceptance of Christianity by educated Indians is not caste, not vaguely "nationalism," not the Brahmin's pride, but just this—profound conviction that the churches as a whole are more earnest for "edification" than for truth, that to them an experience of spiritual uplifting is more than the righting of a wrong. "This ought ye to have done, and not to leave the other undone."

There is no commoner word on Indian lips to-day than *atonement*. England, they say, has never made atonement; and she must do it before we can be friends. The word in their minds is the Sanskrit *prāyaschitta*, usually translated *atonement*; but its meaning is rather *a gesture*. It is not larger measures of self-government for which they are longing, it is the magnanimous gesture of a great nation, so great that it can afford to admit mistake and wrong-doing, and is too proud to distort facts.

But the last word seems to me this. Seventy years ago our two races were mad, with an awful homicidal insanity. We cannot afford to perpetuate their feud, nor to carry their deeds, which were not ours. That we should probably have shared in them, had we lived when their madness could have drawn us in also, is nothing to the point; it is true of ourselves and of every evil action ever done, the crucifixion of Jesus or the burning of Joan. We can at least refuse to ratify those deeds, or to misrepresent them to flatter our own national esteem. This is a world of fallible men and women, who had no power of choosing their race or land of birth; all we can choose is whether our attitude shall be generous and courageous, or ignoble and cowardly. We who are British can sweep our minds clear of all the poison and untruth that our books have placed there, and we can create an atmosphere in which a new beginning of thought is possible. To many who have read my pages, after the first shock of horror and shame must have come relief, that a monster had been shown to be unreal. Our own madness we can understand, and it is matter for humiliation but not for perplexity; and there is seen to have been no inexplicable

Indian madness, but only the passions of suffering men like ourselves. With such men an understanding is possible, and friendship and forgiveness. And this new attitude, I believe, is the *atonement* that Indians are seeking.

APPENDIX

NOTE ON MUTINY LITERATURE

MEMOIRS are very numerous. Those written some time after the events, when their authors had risen to positions of great distinction and responsibility, are usually reticent and cautious; contemporary documents are written very frankly. But even the most reticent first-hand authorities disclose a very surprising story, and it is no wonder that a great many accounts of the Mutiny ignore original sources, and take over their opinions and summaries ready made.

Many men whose names will never be forgotten in India seem to have kept absolute silence on the deeds which made them memorable there; you can meet their sons to-day, and find that they know nothing of what happened.

Histories of the Mutiny can often be swept aside as second-hand compilation. Many others, whether their authors knew the original documents or not, are garbled throughout — their style is question-begging, inconsequent, insolently self-righteous. Many of these histories have sold very largely, sometimes as reading-matter for boys.

Sir George Trevelyan's *Cawnpore* is the most firmly established as literature of all books on separate phases of the Mutiny. Of reputable histories of the whole episode, Kaye's account of the first year of the war, despite much controversy and attack, remains worthy of respect, as written with full access to first-hand knowledge and with much generosity and fairness. Malleson both contradicts in detail and supplements Kaye's account, and is valuable. Holmes, often praised—but I suspect that Vincent Smith's testimonial is the source of some of the recent praise—is capricious, querulous, illogical, and often downright silly. For example, of the execution of Tantia Tupi: "If he had been as brave as the woman who died fighting on the field from which he ran away, he would have deserved some pity. But, like his master, he was a coward; and posterity will say that his punishment was just"[1] (pp. 533, 534). Well, the Rani of Jhansi, "who died fighting on the field" from which Tantia Tupi "ran away," was killed while trying to escape; and as to what "posterity" will say, my generation—many of whom have been under fire—are part of posterity, and we do not consider a man a coward because he tries to get away from a battle that has become desperate—and Tantia Tupi was fleeing from the gallows as well as from the British arms. Montgomery Martin wrote while the war was dragging to its close, wrote with detailed knowledge and fearlessness of judgment; I consider him on the whole much the best historian. Sir George Forrest's *History of the Indian Mutiny* is a very large book. Sir George Campbell's *Memoirs of My Indian Career* contains a valuable account and

[1] Tantia Tupi was hanged not for cowardice but—by a sentence whose legality was doubtful—for treason. That is why posterity is invited to condemn him for reasons which would be irrelevant, even if true.

discussion of the Mutiny. Russell's *Diary* is very important.

Perhaps the most contemptible of all histories of the Mutiny is *The Tale of the Great Mutiny*, by the Rev. W. H. Fitchett, LL.D. Its sales and influence have been very great.

Vincent Smith (*Oxford History of India*, p. 731) remarks of the Mutiny: "Numerous incidents are the subject of controversy, and the evidence often is conflicting." Not only so; many of the larger issues, as to how far the Mutiny was a genuine war of independence, as to what, if any, outside fomenting helped to bring it about, as to how far it was preconcerted, the experiences of the Indian leaders—especially during its last phase of arduous, guerilla warfare in hill and jungle—and its lasting effects, have never been competently or dispassionately handled. It has been chronicled from one side only, and from one set of documents; or from no documents at all, but mere stereotyped hearsay.

PERSONAL NOTES

The following personal notes on writers or actors referred to in my pages may help the reader to judge of the degree of authority or importance attaching to each. No note is needed on such names as John Lawrence or Nicholson. I have compiled these notes chiefly from the *Dictionary of National Biography*, Buckland's *Dictionary of Indian Biography*, and *Who's Who*.

APPENDIX

CAMPBELL, SIR GEORGE, 1824–92. I.C.S., 1842; Assisted Colvin in the government of the North-West Provinces, and became Commissioner of the Cis-Satlej States, 1855; Provisional Civil Commissioner in the Mutiny; wrote letters on the Mutiny to the *Times*, and an official account of it for Lord Canning; Judge of the High Court, Calcutta, 1862; Chief Commissioner, Central Provinces, November 1867; D.C.L., Oxford, 1870; Lieut.-Governor, Bengal, 1871–74; K.C.S.I., 1873; M.P., Kirkcaldy, 1875–92. Author: *Modern India, The Ethnology of India, The Capital of India, Tenure of Land in India, The Eastern Question*, etc.

COTTON, SIR HENRY JOHN STEDMAN, 1845–1915. I.C.S., 1867; Secretary, Revenue Department, Bengal Government, 1888; Financial Department, 1889; Chief Secretary, 1891–96; Acting Home Secretary, Government of India, 1896; Chief Commissioner, Assam, 1896–1902; K.C.S.I., 1902; President, Indian National Congress, 1904; M.P., East Nottingham, 1906. Author: *Memorandum on the Revenue History of Chittagong, Memorandum on the Land Tenure of Bengal, New India, Indian and Home Memories.*

DUTT, ROMESHCHANDRA, 1848–1909. I.C.S., 1871; Magistrate, Backerganj, 1883 ("the first Indian to receive executive charge of a district since the establishment of British rule."—*D.N.B.*); Acting Divisional Commissioner, Burdwan, 1894–95 ("the only Indian to rise to executive charge of a division in the nineteenth century."—*D.N.B.*); Barrister, Middle Temple; Lecturer on Indian History,

University College, London, 1898–1904; Revenue Minister, Baroda State, 1904–1907; Prime Minister, Baroda, 1909. Author: many novels, etc., in Bengali, and in English of translations of the *Ramayana* and *Mahabbarata*, *Lays of Ancient India*, *Economic History of British India*, *Civilisation in Ancient India*, *India in the Victorian Age*, *Lake of Palms*.

FITCHETT, REV. WILLIAM HENRY. LL.D., Toronto; Principal, Methodist Ladies' College, Melbourne; President, Wesleyan Conference, Victoria and Tasmania; President, General Conference, Methodist Church of Australasia. Author: *Deeds that Won the Empire*, *Fights for the Flag*, *The Tale of the Great Mutiny*, *How England Saved Europe*, *Wellington's Men*, *Nelson and His Captains*, *The Commander of the Hirondelle*, *The Unrealised Logic of Religion*, *Life of Wesley*, *Ithuriel's Spear*, *The Beliefs of Unbelief*, etc.

FORREST, SIR GEORGE WILLIAM, 1846–. Son of Captain George Forrest, V.C., one of the tiny band whose almost incredible heroism saved the magazine at Delhi from falling intact into the hands of the mutineers; Bombay Educational Department, 1872; Census Commissioner, Bombay, 1882; Professor, English History, Elphinstone College, Bombay, 1887; Director, Bombay Records, 1888; Director, Government of India Records, 1894–1900; C.I.E., 1899. Author: *The Administration of Warren Hastings*, *The Administration of Lord Lansdowne*, *Sepoy Generals*, several series of *Selections from State Papers relating to Indian*

History, including two volumes relating to the Mutiny, *Cities of India, Lord Clive, History of the Indian Mutiny*, etc.

FORSYTH, SIR THOMAS DOUGLAS, 1827–86. I.C.S., Calcutta, 1848; Punjab, 1849; Deputy Commissioner, Umballa, on outbreak of the Mutiny; a Special Commissioner for punishing the rebels, after fall of Delhi; Secretary to Chief Commissioner, Oudh; C.B.; on diplomatic missions on the frontier and in Russia; Envoy to Yarkand, 1870; lost his post as Commissioner, Umballa, 1872; led a mission to Kashgar, 1873–74; K.C.S.I., 1874; Additional Member of Governor-General's Legislative Council, 1874; Envoy to Burma, 1875. Author: *Autobiography and Reminiscences.*

HOLMES, THOMAS RICE EDWARD, 1855–. Master, Lincoln Grammar School, 1878–80; Blackheath Proprietary School, 1880–85; Master, St Paul's School, 1886–1909. Author: *A History of the Indian Mutiny*, 1883 (5th edition, revised, 1898, twice reprinted since), *Four Famous Soldiers, Cæsar's Conquest of Gaul*, etc.

KAYE, SIR JOHN WILLIAM, 1814–76. Bengal Artillery, 1832–33; retired, to practise literature, 1841; established *Calcutta Review*, 1844; entered Home Civil Service of East India Company, 1856; succeeded John Stuart Mill as Secretary in the Political and Secret Department, India Office, 1858; K.C.S.I., 1871; F.R.S. Author: *History of the War in Afghanistan, Administration of the East India Company, Life and Correspondence of Lord*

Metcalfe, Life of Henry St George Tucker, Life of Sir John Malcolm, Christianity in India, History of the Sepoy War, Lives of Indian Officers, etc.

MALLESON, GEORGE BRUCE, 1825–98. Bengal Native Infantry, 1844; Second Burmese War, 1852–53; wrote anonymously *The Mutiny of the Bengal Army* (in which he blamed Dalhousie's administration and especially the annexation of Oudh as responsible—this was published in 1857, and known as "the red pamphlet"); Sanitary Commissioner, Bengal, 1866–68; Controller, Military Finance Department, 1868–69; Guardian of the young Maharaja of Mysore, 1869–77; C.S.I., 1872; Colonel, 1873. Author: *Essays and Lectures on Indian Historical Subjects, History of the French in India, Recreations of an Indian Official, Historical Sketch of the Native States of India, Final French Struggles in India and on the Indian Seas, History of the Indian Mutiny, History of Afghanistan, Herat, Lord Clive* (in "Founders of the Indian Empire"), *The Decisive Battles of India, The Russo-Afghan Question and the Invasion of India, Wellesley, Akbar, Dupleix, Warren Hastings*, etc.

MARTIN, ROBERT MONTGOMERY, 1803 ?–68. In Ceylon and India as surgeon, botanist, naturalist, 1820–30; Member of the Court of Directors, East India Company; Treasurer, Hong-Kong, 1844–45; one of the first Members of the East India Association, 1866. Author: *The History of the British Colonies, History of the Antiquities of Eastern India, The Marquis of Wellesley's Despatches, The Monetary*

System of British India, The Indian Empire, The Rise and Progress of the Indian Mutiny (published 1859).

METCALFE, SIR THEOPHILUS JOHN, Bart., 1828–83. Born at Delhi; I.C.S., 1848; made his home in India, removing all his possessions to a magnificent house in Delhi, where he had the best library in India (completely destroyed in the Mutiny); Magistrate in Delhi when the Mutiny broke out; acted with great courage and promptitude, and afterwards had an astounding and perilous escape; in the siege of Delhi, showed reckless bravery as a guide; foremost in what Malleson calls the "retributive eagerness of the civilians." Montgomery Martin observes: "It was right to resort to Sir T. Metcalfe as a witness, but not also as a judge. It is contrary to English ideas of justice that a man should be suffered to carry out his notions of retribution by hanging as many victims as he pleases on the beams and angles of his ruined house." C.B., 1864.

MONTGOMERY, SIR ROBERT, 1809–87. I.C.S., 1828; Commissioner, Lahore, 1849; Judicial Commissioner, 1853; Chief Commissioner, Oudh, 1858; Lieut.-Governor, Punjab, 1859–January 1865; K.C.B., 1859; G.C.S.I., 1866; Member of the Council of India, 1868–87. The Montgomery Hall at Lahore was erected as a memorial to him. "His chief characteristics were insatiable industry, cool decision, kindness of heart, and personal modesty" (*D.N.B.*). Author: *Abstract Principles of Law for the Use of Civil Administrative Officers.*

RUSSELL, SIR WILLIAM HOWARD, 1820–1907. The greatest of war correspondents; *Times*, Crimea, Indian Mutiny, Italy, United States Civil War, Prusso-Austro-Danish War, Austro-Prussian War, Franco-German War, South African Wars of 1879–80 and 1883–84; accompanied Prince of Wales on Indian Tour, 1875–76; Editor, *Army and Navy Gazette*; F.R.G.S.; F.Z.S. Author: *Letters from the Crimea, British Expedition to the Crimea, Diary in India, Diary—North and South, Diary in the Last Great War, Hesperothen, Adventures of Dr Brady, A Retrospect of the Crimea, Todleben's Sebastopol*, etc.

SMITH, VINCENT ARTHUR, 1848–1920. I.C.S., 1871; after much experience of settlement work in the North-West Provinces and Oudh, Collector, 1889; District Judge, 1895; Chief Secretary, 1898; Commissioner, 1898; Reader in Indian History and Hindustani, Dublin University, 1902–1903. Author: *The Settlement Officer's Manual for the N.W.P., General Index to Cunningham's Archæological Survey Reports, The Remains Near Kasia, The Jain Stupa and Other Antiquities of Mathura, Asoka, Akbar, The Early History of India, Catalogue of the Non-Muhammadan Coins in the Indian Museum, Oxford History of India*, etc. From both his experiences in the districts which had suffered during the Mutiny and his study of Mutiny documents, he obviously developed a great distaste for the whole subject, and would have preferred to see it passed over as lightly as possible in our histories; but in every country public opinion, on certain deeply cherished episodes, demands that historians continually reassure and flatter it by repetition of what it expects to hear, because it always has heard it. If my English readers refuse to admit that this is true of our own public opinion, they will at any rate admit that it is true of foreign public opinion—when Americans write about their Revolution or the French about Napoleon or Germans about the Great War. My regard for Vincent Smith's work and character is so great that I write these sentences with regret, as explanation of those statements of his which I have censured—their presence in his moderately written account of the Mutiny shows how overwhelming is the pressure of outside expectation, forcing even a conscientious writer into things he would rather not have said. Or so it seems to me. There is the same explanation (I think) for Sir George Forrest's lapses from the high standard he announced in his "Preface."